PROJECT
BASED
TEACHING

ASCD MEMBER BOOK

Many ASCD members received this book as a
member benefit upon its initial release.

Learn more at: **www.ascd.org/memberbooks**

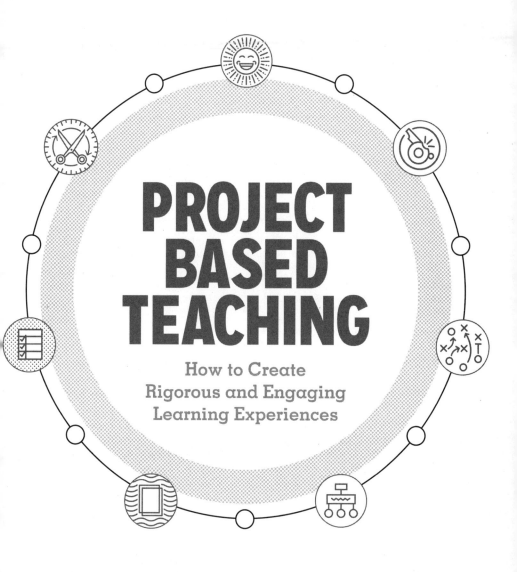

PROJECT BASED TEACHING

How to Create Rigorous and Engaging Learning Experiences

SUZIE BOSS WITH **JOHN LARMER**

FOREWORD BY BOB LENZ

ASCD

ALEXANDRIA, VA USA

BIE

BUCK INSTITUTE
FOR EDUCATION

1703 N. Beauregard St. • Alexandria, VA 22311-1714 USA
Phone: 800-933-2723 or 703-578-9600 • Fax: 703-575-5400
Website: www.ascd.org • E-mail: member@ascd.org
Author guidelines: www.ascd.org/write

Buck Institute for Education
18 Commercial Blvd.
Novato, CA 94949 USA

Deborah S. Delisle, *Executive Director;* Stefani Roth, *Publisher;* Genny Ostertag, *Director, Content Acquisitions;* Julie Houtz, *Director, Book Editing & Production;* Jamie Greene, *Associate Editor;* Judi Connelly, *Associate Art Director;* Donald Ely, *Senior Graphic Designer;* Valerie Younkin, *Senior Production Designer;* Mike Kalyan, *Director, Production Services;* Shajuan Martin, *E-Publishing Specialist*

All web links in this book are correct as of the publication date below but may have become inactive or otherwise modified since that time. If you notice a deactivated or changed link, please e-mail books@ascd.org with the words "Link Update" in the subject line. In your message, please specify the web link, the book title, and the page number on which the link appears.

PAPERBACK ISBN: 978-1-4166-2673-2   ASCD product #118047
PDF E-BOOK ISBN: 978-1-4166-2675-6; see Books in Print for other formats.

Quantity discounts: 10–49, 10%; 50+, 15%; 1,000+, special discounts (e-mail programteam@ascd.org or call 800-933-2723, ext. 5773, or 703-575-5773). For desk copies, go to www.ascd.org/deskcopy.

ASCD Member Book No. F19-1 (Sep. 2018 PSI+). ASCD Member Books mail to Premium (P), Select (S), and Institutional Plus (I+) members on this schedule: Jan, PSI+; Feb, P; Apr, PSI+; May, P; Jul, PSI+; Aug, P; Sep, PSI+; Nov, PSI+; Dec, P. For current details on membership, see www.ascd.org/membership.

Library of Congress Cataloging-in-Publication Data
Names: Boss, Suzie, author. | Larmer, John, author.
Title: Project based teaching : how to create rigorous and engaging learning experiences / Suzie Boss with John Larmer.
Description: Alexandria, VA : ASCD ; Novato, CA : Buck Institute for Education, [2018] | Includes bibliographical references and index.
Identifiers: LCCN 2018023357 (print) | LCCN 2018026545 (ebook) | ISBN 9781416626756 (PDF) | ISBN 9781416626732 (pbk.)
Subjects: LCSH: Project method in teaching. | Effective teaching.
Classification: LCC LB1027.43 (ebook) | LCC LB1027.43 .B65 2018 (print) | DDC 371.3/6--dc23
LC record available at https://lccn.loc.gov/2018023357

26 25 24 23 22 21 20 19 18   1 2 3 4 5 6 7 8 9 10 11 12

To the talented and dedicated National Faculty
of the Buck Institute for Education

PROJECT BASED

TEACHING

Acknowledgments ix

Foreword by Bob Lenz xi

Introduction 1

1   Build the Culture 11

2   Design and Plan 38

3   Align to Standards 67

4   Manage Activities 80

5   Assess Student Learning 104

6   Scaffold Student Learning 127

7   Engage and Coach 157

8   Closing Reflections 176

Appendix:

   Project Based Teaching Rubric 180

   Student Learning Guide 187

References 192

Index 197

About the Authors 206

Acknowledgments

This book would not have been possible without the contributions of many talented and thoughtful educators.

John Mergendoller laid the foundation when he promoted the need to focus on the role of the teacher in Project Based Learning (PBL) and collaborated with John Larmer to conceptualize the Gold Standard PBL model's Essential Project Design Elements and the Project Based Teaching Practices. Mergendoller's insightful feedback on early drafts of this book helped us keep the focus on what matters most for high-quality teaching and learning.

Dozens more individuals shared practical strategies, informed by extensive classroom experiences. In particular, we are indebted to the Buck Institute for Education (BIE) National Faculty. These educators, working in diverse contexts across the United States (and beyond), live and breathe PBL every day as teachers, instructional coaches, school leaders, and professional development experts. Their suggestions and insights can be found in every chapter.

BIE staff shaped the book in significant ways, from early brainstorming to critique and review of draft chapters. Many of the tools and strategies featured in the book are the result of staff creativity and collaboration, particularly by Sarah Field and Gina Olabuenaga, who manage the creation of BIE's PBL 201 workshops.

We owe special thanks to seven teachers who opened their classrooms for close observation and reflection while projects were

underway with students. Their stories and advice are woven throughout this book and also captured in a companion set of videos. Featured
teachers include Telannia Norfar, Ray Ahmed, Rebecca Newburn, Erin
Brandvold, Sara Lev, Kimberly Head-Trotter, and Cheryl Bautista.

We learned more about Project Based Teaching from dozens
of interviews and blog posts shared by these PBL veterans: Feroze
Munshi, Sherry Griesinger, Myla Lee, Abby Schneiderjohn, Erin Gan-
non, Ian Stevenson, Brandon Cohen, Julia Cagle, Tom Lee, Eric White,
Krystal Diaz, Jim Bentley, Meghan Ashkanani, Mike Gwaltney, Dara
Laws Savage, Mike Kaechele, Kevin Gant, James Fester, Tyler Millsap,
Scott Stephen Bell, Kelly Reseigh, Tom Neville, Andrew Miller, John
McCarthy, Kristin Uliasz, Erin Starkey, Heather Wolpert-Gawron, and
Brian Schoch. Forgive us for any omissions.

Equity is a theme that permeates this book. It's our shared belief
that all students, regardless of ZIP code, deserve opportunities for the
meaningful, engaging learning that happens in Gold Standard PBL.
We thank the many fellow travelers, too numerous to list here, who
are creating transformative learning opportunities for their students.

Finally, we thank editor Genny Ostertag and her team at ASCD
for encouraging us to bring this book to readers.

Foreword

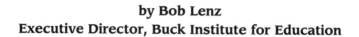

by Bob Lenz
Executive Director, Buck Institute for Education

The world has changed dramatically over the last generation—even over the last 10 years. Our lives have become far more connected through technology, a global economy, and social media. Our awareness of the complexity of the challenges we face as human beings—from climate change to issues of conflict and food distribution—has grown substantially. The world of work is changing rapidly, too. More and more tasks are being automated—from manufacturing to driving to writing data-based reports. Furthermore, collaboration has become the norm; most people in Information Age companies work in and across teams. Finally, it has become a project-based world. Forty percent of people in the United States work as contract employees, moving from one client's project to another. This is expected to grow to 60 percent by 2025. Almost all work, even in traditional companies, is organized by projects. Given the dramatic changes in the world, one would think that schools have also changed. Yet, for the most part, we educate our youth the same way we did over 100 years ago.

Over the last three years, I have had the opportunity to ask people all over the world—young and old, educators and business leaders, community leaders and parents—this question: "Given the changes in the world, what skills and dispositions are needed for success?" Amazingly, no matter where I asked the question, among all groups, I found consensus on the answer. In addition to academic content knowledge and skills, students need success skills such as collaboration, communication (oral, written, and visual), critical thinking and problem solving, project management and self-management, creativity and innovation, and a sense of empowerment to tackle the challenges of their lives and our world. The students experiencing the kind of Project Based Learning described in this book are gaining these skills and dispositions.

The Need for Project Based Teaching

Though we all agree that the world has changed, we also know that schools have not. With this growing awareness, we have started to see some shifts around the United States and globally. We see schools and districts working toward more student-centered approaches that include inquiry learning, personalized learning, performance-based assessments, and a huge surge of interest in and implementation of Project Based Learning. To meet the demand for examples of projects and PBL professional development for teachers, the field has responded.

Examples of high-quality projects can be found in many places, and due to the excellent work of my colleagues at the Buck Institute for Education and other education organizations focused on deeper learning, teachers can access materials, resources, and workshops on how to *design* high-quality projects. The Essential Project Design Elements in the Buck Institute's model for Gold Standard PBL, first described in *Setting the Standard for Project Based Learning* (Larmer, Mergendoller, & Boss, 2015), have been well received and adopted by educators across the country and around the world. The Project Based Teaching Practices also introduced in that book have equally resonated with the field; however, more is needed about how to *teach* in a PBL classroom.

Educators need detailed descriptions, strategies, and video so they can learn about the teacher moves that lead to effective implementation of PBL. *Project Based Teaching*, plus a series of videos released by the Buck Institute for Education (available at www.bie.

org), answers this call by highlighting the work of seven diverse and successful PBL teachers. Several more teachers are heard from in this book, many of whom are in the Buck Institute's National Faculty. These teachers are not necessarily the "rock stars" you might see in popular movies; they are regular folks who are nonetheless inspirational for their classroom skills, depth of knowledge, and passion for doing a good job for all kids.

How School and District Leaders Create the Conditions for Project Based Teaching

Whereas *Project Based Teaching* focuses on the nitty-gritty of how teachers facilitate high-quality learning experiences for students, the work of school and district leaders to put the conditions in place for teachers to do great projects with kids cannot be overlooked. In the schools where we see excellent implementation of Project Based Learning, we also find

- **A clear, coherent, and compelling vision for new goals for education and new ways of teaching and learning.** Leaders work with staff and community stakeholders to establish a vision that includes a graduate profile with 21st century success skills and explicitly calls for Project Based Learning experiences as the method for reaching that goal.
- **A culture of learning, innovation, and inquiry for students, teachers, and leaders.** Leaders make it safe for teachers to innovate and take risks. This is reflected in the classroom practice of PBL. The school poses questions about its work and follows an inquiry process to answer them, much like students do in a project.
- **Redesigned and reimagined school structures.** For example, the master schedule is modified to allow for longer, more flexible blocks of instructional time; teachers are provided with more individual and collaborative planning and learning time; middle and high schools organize students into cohort groups where teams of teachers share the same students.

- **Deep and consistent capacity building for teachers and the leadership team.** The teachers we learn from in *Project Based Teaching* have all had professional development workshops, ongoing instructional coaching, and collaborative planning opportunities to hone their craft.
- **A commitment to continuous improvement.** One learns how to facilitate high-quality Project Based Learning by facilitating Project Based Learning. I am sure all of the teachers in this book would tell you that their strategies and effectiveness have improved dramatically from their first PBL unit. By employing the Essential Project Design Element of critique and revision, like students do in a project, they continue to improve their practice of PBL.

How This Book Reflects the Framework for High-Quality PBL

In 2018, a steering committee of 27 educators and thought leaders with a stake in Project Based Learning, plus representatives of organizations that prominently feature PBL in their programs, finalized a Framework for High-Quality PBL that describes what high-quality Project Based Learning looks like in terms of the student experience. The steering committee also included international representation from Finland, Chile, South Korea, and China. The purpose of the Framework is to create a shared agreement (which did not previously exist) about what high-quality PBL is to guide the work of teachers, schools, academics, education leaders, policymakers, journalists, and curriculum and service providers.

The effort was facilitated by the Buck Institute for Education, partnered with Getting Smart and with support from the Project Management Institute Educational Foundation and the William and Flora Hewlett Foundation. The development of the Framework took 12 months and was a highly collaborative and iterative process, with substantial input from the public, teachers, and other organizations.

Here are the six criteria in the Framework for High-Quality PBL that must be present to some extent in order for a project to be judged as high quality. (Visit https://hqpbl.org for more details, including the research behind these six criteria.)

Intellectual Challenge and Accomplishment

Students learn deeply, think critically, and strive for excellence. To what extent do students

- Investigate challenging problems, questions, and issues over an extended period of time?
- Focus on concepts, knowledge, and skills central to subject areas and intellectual disciplines?
- Experience research-based instruction and support as needed for learning and project success?
- Commit themselves to completing work of the highest quality?

Authenticity

Students work on projects that are meaningful and relevant to their culture, their lives, and their future. To what extent do students

- Engage in work that connects to the world beyond school and to their personal interests and concerns?
- Use the tools, techniques, and/or digital technologies employed in the world beyond school?
- Make choices regarding project topics, activities, and/or products?

Public Product

Students' work is publicly displayed, discussed, and critiqued. To what extent do students

- Exhibit their work and describe their learning to peers and people beyond the classroom?

- Receive feedback and/or engage in dialogue with their audiences?

Collaboration

Students collaborate with other students in person or online and/or receive guidance from adult mentors and experts. To what extent do students

- Work in teams to complete complex tasks?
- Learn to become effective team members and leaders?
- Learn how to work with adult mentors, experts, community members, businesses, and organizations?

Project Management

Students use a project management process that enables them to proceed effectively from project initiation to completion. To what extent do students

- Manage themselves and their teams efficiently and effectively throughout a multistep project?
- Learn to use project management processes, tools, and strategies?
- Use the perspectives and processes of design thinking, as appropriate?

Reflection

Students reflect on their work and their learning throughout the project. To what extent do students

- Learn to assess and suggest improvements in their own and other students' work?
- Reflect on, write about, and discuss the academic content, concepts, and success skills they are learning?
- Use reflection as a tool to increase their own personal agency?

When the Framework for High-Quality Project Based Learning was announced, educators and organizations across the United States and around the world signed on to register their commitment to it, joining an effort that continues to gather momentum today. Everyone who commits might have different ways to turn the vision described by the Framework into reality for students. In the case of the Buck Institute, it's our model for Gold Standard PBL, as described in *Setting the Standard for Project Based Learning* and in this book. The teaching practices and project designs showcased in *Project Based Teaching* will result in "yes" answers to all of the questions posed by the six criteria.

The vision of the Buck Institute for Education is that all students, no matter where they are from or what their background, have the opportunity to experience high-quality Project Based Learning. We believe that, when done well, Project Based Learning serves as a tool for educational equity by empowering students to learn the academic content and skills plus the success skills they will need to meet the challenges in their lives and in our world. We hope that *Project Based Teaching* and the accompanying video series help build the capacity of teachers everywhere and at all educational levels to design and facilitate great projects for their students—including those furthest from opportunity.

Onward with love and purpose,

Bob Lenz
Executive Director
Buck Institute for Education
February 2018

Introduction

Every aspect of school change depends on highly skilled teachers for its success.
—Linda Darling-Hammond

There's no question that Project Based Learning (PBL) is gaining traction as a key instructional strategy, both across the United States and around the globe. Reasons for introducing PBL are numerous and can differ from one school system to the next. Across a wide range of contexts, however, there's growing recognition that today's complex world puts new demands on students as they prepare for college, careers, and active citizenship. Those demands won't be met without a fundamental shift away from traditional, teacher-centered instruction and toward more innovative, student-centered teaching and learning.

For schools ready to make that shift, PBL offers a proven framework to help students be better equipped to tackle future challenges. Through academically rigorous projects, students acquire deep content knowledge while also mastering 21st century success skills: knowing how to think critically, analyze information for reliability, collaborate with diverse colleagues, and solve problems creatively. In the process of engaging with PBL, students learn to ask good questions, be resourceful, manage their time, meet authentic deadlines, and persist through challenges. When done well, PBL fosters self-management and self-directed learning. These are precisely the competencies that will enable students to thrive in the future they will help shape.

Along with new demands on students come fresh challenges for educators. Relatively few teachers had the chance to experience PBL as students when they were younger, and teacher preparation programs are only just starting to include PBL methods. Without prior experience or professional training, many teachers face a steep learning curve. They may wonder if introducing PBL means starting from scratch with lesson planning, assessment, and daily classroom routines. They worry whether they will be able to cover the required curriculum if they make time for PBL. Newcomers to PBL often ask, "What changes with PBL? What stays the same in my classroom? And how do I know if I'm doing it right?"

The Buck Institute for Education (BIE) has helped thousands of teachers gain confidence with PBL through face-to-face workshops, and online resources and books have reached countless more educators around the globe. *Setting the Standard for Project Based Learning* (Larmer, Mergendoller, & Boss, 2015) was written in response to the groundswell of interest in PBL. The goal with that book was to help teachers and school leaders design and implement PBL *well*, regardless of their location or school context. Students from every ZIP code and background deserve to benefit from high-quality PBL experiences.

Setting the Standard for Project Based Learning introduced a framework for Gold Standard PBL. Informed by research and extensive input from teachers and school leaders, the Gold Standard sets a high bar when it comes to academic rigor. That's important, because poorly executed PBL can be a waste of valuable learning time. We've seen too many so-called projects that focus on fun and hands-on activities but fail to address significant learning goals. When PBL is done well, on the other hand, the stage is set for a deep dive into meaningful academic content. Project Based Learning involves sustained inquiry into challenging questions or problems. Students need to not only learn content but also be able to apply it. By definition, Gold Standard PBL is "main course" learning—not dessert.

To accomplish consistently deep and meaningful learning, Gold Standard PBL calls for seven Essential Project Design Elements (see Figure 0.1):

- Challenging problem or question
- Sustained inquiry
- Authenticity
- Student voice and choice
- Reflection
- Critique and revision
- Public product

Figure 0.1 Essential Project Design Elements for Gold Standard PBL

Emphasizing these elements from start to finish in a project helps ensure that the learning experience will be worth the investment by students and teachers alike. These elements set the stage for project success whether you use PBL all the time or only occasionally during the school year.

Setting the Standard for Project Based Learning also introduced a set of seven Project Based Teaching Practices but did not explore them in depth. Feedback from teachers, school leaders, and instructional coaches indicates a desire for more. Educators shifting to PBL want more examples of high-quality projects in action. They want to see not just final, polished results of student learning but more of the day-to-day instructional practices that teachers use along the way to support and engage all students in this type of learning. They want to hear other teachers' strategies for making enough time and space for PBL within their curriculum. This book and a related series of free videos provide a much more detailed look at what's happening in PBL classrooms from the perspective of the Project Based Teacher (see www.bie.org).

Project Based Teaching Practices

For students to succeed with PBL, teachers may have to make major shifts in instructional practice. This is especially true for those who have taught in traditional settings, relying primarily on direct instruction, textbooks, and tests. Instead of being the all-knowing expert who transmits knowledge, the PBL teacher is a well-informed coach, facilitator of learning, and guide through the inquiry process. Rather than holding all the answers, Project Based Teachers encourage active questioning, curiosity, and peer learning. They create learning environments in which every student has a voice. They have a mastery of content but are also comfortable responding to students' questions by saying, "I don't know. Let's find out together." (See Figure 0.2.)

The shift to Project Based Teaching often happens gradually as teachers identify and adopt strategies that help their students succeed. Unless you are teaching in a wall-to-wall PBL school, where students are consistently learning through projects in every content area, you will likely alternate between PBL and more traditional instruction throughout the school year. For example, many teachers set a realistic goal of doing at least two projects per semester.

Personalized learning, an increasingly popular trend in education, is compatible with and shares many student-centered instructional practices with PBL. Although PBL acknowledges the importance of student voice and choice, personalized learning puts even more of a premium on students' individual interests, skills, and developmental needs (Jobs for the Future & the Council of Chief State School Officers, 2015).

Schools that focus on personalized learning also tend to emphasize a competency-based progression toward mastery of content and skills. They may make use of individual learner profiles that describe each student's strengths and areas for growth, or they may award badges for mastery of specific competencies. In addition, students may have time built into their regular class schedules to pursue individual interests through passion projects or "Genius Hour" experiences. To encourage personalization, schools may use a blended learning approach—combining face-to-face instruction with online learning—to give students more control over when, where, and how they learn. Some schools are also exploring a combination of personalized learning and PBL—with students pursuing individual interests for part of the day and taking part in more collaborative, standards-based projects at other times.

Figure 0.2   Project Based Teaching Practices for Gold Standard PBL

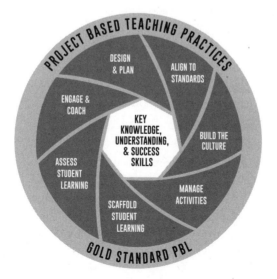

Regardless of whether projects are done by teams or individually, if the projects are of high quality—with teachers paying attention to Project Based Teaching Practices—all of these PBL experiences have the potential to be high points of the school year for you and your students.

In the chapters ahead, you will gain insights into each of the seven Project Based Teaching Practices that support student success. For each practice, you will discover a wide range of practical strategies and hear teachers reflect about their classroom experiences. Just as student voice is essential to high-quality PBL, teacher choice is embedded in effective Project Based Teaching.

Build the Culture: Classroom culture conveys an ethic of care, an emphasis on excellence, and a sense of shared intention. The right culture builds students' independence, fosters collaboration, encourages a growth mindset, supports risk taking, encourages high-quality work, and builds inclusiveness and equity. In many ways, culture is the fuel for student voice and choice, sustained inquiry, and persistence. Positive culture doesn't get built with a one-day team builder. It's an ongoing effort to create an inclusive community of learners.

Design and Plan: Intentional design of the learning experience sets the stage for students and teachers to capitalize on the full potential of PBL. Essential Project Design Elements provide a blueprint for the project, including planning for both formative and summative assessment. Teacher decisions at the design stage include curating resources and, potentially, connecting with experts or community partners. Project Based Learning plans allow room for student voice and choice but keep the project from becoming unwieldy.

Align to Standards: By aligning projects to meaningful learning goals, teachers ensure that PBL is academically rigorous and has an emphasis on priority standards and higher-order thinking. What's more, students understand *why* they're learning what they're learning and how PBL relates to the world beyond the classroom.

Manage Activities: A well-managed PBL experience enables students to get to deep learning and develop the teamwork and self-management skills that will serve them in life. Project management strategies focus on productivity and efficiency, but PBL is not about following a recipe. A well-managed project allows for sometimes "messy" learning.

Assess Student Learning: Assessment ensures that students work toward mastery. It's not about "gotchas" or sorting but about growth. PBL requires a balance of formative and summative assessment, including both team and individual feedback. Feedback comes from multiple sources, including peers, experts, and audiences along with the teacher. Students have time to improve and refine their work based on comprehensive feedback.

Scaffold Student Learning: Scaffolding creates conditions so every student can succeed with the project and master learning goals. In an equitable classroom, students' prior learning experiences, language fluency, or reading levels are not barriers to success.

Engage and Coach: Engaging and coaching strategies bring out the best in students. Coaching strategies use questioning, modeling, and reflection to build intrinsic motivation and help students achieve their learning goals. A caring, trusting relationship between teacher and students is the foundation for successful PBL.

The closing chapter offers advice and reflections from teachers who have made the shift to PBL. Their experiences show us that PBL gets better with practice. Becoming a skilled Project Based Teacher doesn't happen with one project; it's an ongoing process of professional learning, supported by effective school leaders, instructional coaches, and teaching colleagues. Although many day-to-day classroom practices do change with a shift to PBL, teachers are often relieved to discover that they can make effective use of tried-and-true resources and strategies within the context of PBL.

What doesn't change with the introduction of PBL is the critical importance of a caring teacher in the lives of students. Indeed, when teachers begin to implement PBL, they often say that they get to know their students better as a result. A common refrain among teachers who have made the shift to PBL is "Doing projects with my students reminds me why I went into teaching in the first place."

Meet the Teachers

Project Based Teachers from across the United States have opened their classrooms for this book and for the companion series of videos. They teach across grade levels and content areas, and they work in schools that vary widely when it comes to student demographics and socioeconomics. You will hear them describe how they use specific Project Based Teaching Practices to support student learning. Unless otherwise indicated, their stories are based on interviews or personal correspondence with the authors or video crew.

Teachers whose stories are woven throughout this book include a math teacher from an urban high school, an elementary teacher whose students include a number of English language learners, a suburban middle school science teacher who wants her students to become well-informed citizens, a chemistry teacher in a high school where a high percentage of students have special needs, and many more. Some teachers work with students who will be the first in their families to attend college. Advocates for educational equity, these teachers see PBL as the best way to prepare *all* learners for the future. You will hear, too, from instructional coaches who play important supporting roles in helping Project Based Teachers build their confidence with new strategies.

Across different contexts, these educators share a belief that their students will rise to the challenges of PBL. High expectations for all are an integral part of the PBL culture. As one high school humanities teacher regularly tells her students, "I believe in you."

Special Features

This book also includes special features to deepen your understanding of Project Based Teaching Practices and strategies to help PBL take hold in your community:

- **Gold Standard Indicators:** Each chapter describes what Gold Standard Project Based Teaching Practices should look like in action, with indicators from the Buck Institute for

Education's Project Based Teaching Rubric (included in full in the Appendix).

- **Try This:** Watch for these descriptions of activities to support PBL in your context. Try these ideas with your students and colleagues and then reflect on the results.
- **Coaches' Notebook:** How can instructional coaches and teacher leaders support PBL? Veteran coaches offer suggestions to improve practice and build teachers' confidence with Project Based Teaching.
- **On Your PBL Bookshelf:** Recommended readings are offered to deepen your understanding of each Project Based Teaching Practice.

Appendix

The Appendix includes two more resources that will help you continue to develop your capacity as a Project Based Teacher.

- **Project Based Teaching Rubric:** The complete rubric for Project Based Teaching Practices is included for reference. A continuum of criteria is included for each of the seven practices for the Beginning PBL Teacher, the Developing PBL Teacher, and the Gold Standard PBL Teacher. Intended as a tool for professional growth, the rubric is a useful tool for self-reflection, in professional development, or as part of collegial conversations about PBL.
- **Sample of Completed Student Learning Guide:** Teachers make many design decisions to set the stage for Gold Standard PBL. To help readers envision the planning involved in an academically rigorous project, the Appendix includes a completed student learning guide for one of the project examples discussed in this book (Revolutions on Trial). To download a blank student learning guide for use in your own project planning, visit www.bie.org and search "Student Learning Guide."

1

Build the Culture

*A positive classroom culture creates an
inclusive community of learners for PBL.*

When Telannia Norfar's high school students arrive for pre-calculus class, they know exactly what to expect. Projected on the screen
at the front of the room are clear instructions for the day's Success
Starter. This three-minute individual activity warms up their thinking
for the learning and project work ahead.

A typical Success Starter might ask students to solve an equation and calculate future college costs. For example:

Using the formula to find the cost for Alia to attend college,
how much will it cost when she is a sophomore? Remember
that Alia is 12 right now.

$A(t) = 17907(1.04)x$

Options:
A $25,487.20
B $24,507.00
C $23,564.40
D $22,658.10

This is not make-believe. These students from Northwest Classen High School in Oklahoma City, Oklahoma, are in the early days of
a project in which they will apply their understanding of exponential,

logarithmic, and rational functions to help real-life clients develop financial plans. They have already met their seven clients whose financial needs include saving for college (in the case of Alia's family), paying for a home mortgage, planning for retirement, or a combination of those factors. Students have started to tackle their driving question: *How can we design financial plans to help our clients meet their needs?*

◼️ A companion video about building the culture for PBL can be found at www.bie.org.

As soon as students complete the warm-up, Norfar outlines the learning objective for the day: "I can create an equation in one variable that represents a financial model and use it to solve a situation."

She asks, "What does this objective mean? What would it mean to know this? How would it help us answer our driving question?" and then instructs students to turn and talk about those questions with their three tablemates.

Students confer for a quick discussion, connecting the new concept to their project goals. Then they regroup with the whole class to hear the teacher introduce a new problem about exponential functions. Norfar gives her students just enough information to get started. They can choose to work on the problem on their own, in collaboration with classmates, or with the support of resources the teacher has made available.

"You might not reach an answer today. You might not reach an answer tomorrow. Struggle is OK," Norfar reminds students as she begins to circulate and observe. Students know that, by the third day, they will be expected to present their understanding and problem-solving strategy to the class.

Conversation starts to build as students discuss the problem and compare strategies. Norfar pauses at the desk of a student who is sitting silent. The girl looks up and confides, "Mrs. Norfar, I'm horrible at math."

"You have a short memory!" she replies with a kind smile. "You say this every time we tackle a problem. Remember last time when you struggled and then overcame your confusion? Remember our norms that we wrote together? One of them was 'We all have a growth mindset.' And remember, I'm here for you."

Why Classroom Culture Matters for PBL

Classroom culture is multifaceted and challenging to define, but it is essential to get right if you want all students to thrive with PBL. Across an entire school, culture encompasses the shared values, beliefs, perceptions, rules (both written and unwritten), and relationships that govern how the institution functions (Çakiroğlu, Akkan, & Güven, 2012; Kane et al., 2016). School culture is also reinforced by norms, expectations, and traditions, including everything from dress codes to discipline systems to celebrations of achievement. Researchers know that students learn best when they feel safe (Scott & Marzano, 2014), and a strong culture encourages effort, supports collaboration, amplifies motivation, and focuses attention on what matters for learning (Deal & Peterson, 2009). A culture that fosters high achievement ensures that the conditions for learning are ever-present and conveys "a shared belief that we are part of something special and great" (Fisher, Frey, & Pumpian, 2012, pp. 6–7).

Indeed, culture is so intertwined with learning that it has been called the hidden curriculum (Jerald, 2006). Sean Slade (2014), an expert on serving the needs of the whole child, argues that culture is shaped by everything that students see, hear, feel, and interact with at school. He elaborates:

> Within a couple of minutes of walking into a school or a classroom, you can tell, define, almost taste the culture that permeates that space. Is it an open, sharing environment? Or is it a rigid, discipline-defined playing field? Is it safe and welcoming, or intimidating and confronting? Does it welcome all voices, or does it make you want to shrink? Is it waiting for instruction and leadership, or is it self-directed with common purpose? (para. 2)

Classroom culture takes on particular significance in PBL. When the goal is to foster inquiry, risk taking, persistence, and self-directed learning, culture is too important to leave to chance. Building the right culture for PBL requires ongoing effort and attention by both teachers and students. Instead of being hidden, a PBL culture needs to be openly constructed, reinforced, and celebrated.

★ Gold Standard Project Based Teaching Indicators: Build the Culture

When a positive culture for learning is established, you should see evidence in how students interact with you and one another. Indicators for building the culture include the following:

- Norms to guide the classroom are cocrafted with and self-monitored by students.

- Student voice and choice is regularly leveraged and ongoing, including identification of real-world issues and problems students want to address in projects.

- Students usually know what they need to do with minimal direction from the teacher.

- Students work collaboratively in healthy, high-functioning teams, much like an authentic work environment; the teacher rarely needs to be involved in managing teams.

- Students understand there is no single "right answer" or preferred way to do the project and that it is OK to take risks, make mistakes, and learn from them.

- The values of critique and revision, persistence, rigorous thinking, and pride in doing high-quality work are shared, and students hold one another accountable to them.

See the Appendix for the complete Project Based Teaching Rubric.

How Teachers (and Students) Shape Culture

Teachers shape culture in both obvious and less noticeable ways. In Norfar's classroom, for example, culture is reflected by the daily Success Starters and other routines, belief in a growth mindset, and even the physical arrangement of the room with students seated in tables of four to foster collaboration. These elements contribute to a welcoming yet academically challenging culture that is built on a foundation of caring relationships.

"My students know I love them," Norfar says, and she regularly underscores that message with her words, gestures, and high expectations. She also doesn't hesitate to mix in some humor.

The teacher's role in building a positive culture is akin to "developing the sorts of attitudes, beliefs, and practices that would characterize a really good neighborhood," according to educational expert Carol Ann Tomlinson (2017, p. 43). Signposts of this kind of classroom "neighborhood" include mutual respect, a sense of safety, an expectation of growth, and a sense that "everyone feels welcomed and contributes to everyone else feeling welcomed" (p. 43).

To find evidence of culture in the classroom, PBL veteran Feroze Munshi suggests looking at your learning environment as if you were an anthropologist. He encourages teachers to consider, "What are the shared attitudes, values, goals, and practices [in your classroom]? What language is used? What are the practices and routines? What artifacts do you see?" All of these components contribute to the culture of learning.

Four Strategies for Building PBL Culture

Let's take a closer look at four culture builders that are especially important for PBL. They involve focusing deliberately on beliefs and values, shared norms, the physical environment, and protocols and routines. For each, a wide range of strategies and classroom traditions will help you and your students build and reinforce a positive PBL culture.

Remember, too, that the right culture for PBL is likely to feel unfamiliar for some students, especially if they have only experienced traditional instruction or top-down discipline in the past. As you introduce more democratic strategies, such as cocreating class norms, talk with students about the purpose and benefits of these activities. Reinforce the message that everyone in the learning community plays an important role in creating and maintaining culture.

Although you will likely put more energy into building culture early in the school year, this needs to be an ongoing effort. Culture building isn't something that happens with just one project, slogan, or team-building activity. Throughout the year, from one project to the next, you'll want to continue reinforcing the values, habits, and routines that contribute to a learning environment in which all students can succeed with PBL.

Ray Ahmed, a high school chemistry teacher at a culturally diverse school in Brooklyn, New York, acknowledges that it takes effort to build and reinforce the right classroom culture for students to succeed with PBL: "We're trying to teach students to be respectful, listen to each other, work together, and have an academic mindset. It's harder in September but so much easier in February when kids are holding each other accountable to the norms."

Beliefs and Values: Sharing What Matters

At the end of every project, Larkspur, California, middle school teacher Rebecca Newburn asks her students for feedback. She reminds them to be kind, specific, and helpful, reflecting their class norms. "I ask them, 'What was helpful? What was not? How was the pacing? Was there too much hands-on or not enough? What helped you learn the most?'"

Once she receives their surveys, she follows up with emails to individual students. "I might say, 'I really like your feedback about the pacing of the project. Can you tell me more? What would have been better?'"

Students are often surprised by her response. "They'll say, 'Oh, my gosh, you actually listened!' I'm modeling that listening to their feedback adds to the culture. I'm showing them that they really do have a voice." Being transparent about what you value helps students see you as a partner in learning and a supporter in their PBL endeavors. Teachers share their beliefs and values with students directly and through action.

Math teacher Telannia Norfar, for example, reminds students that she believes they all can succeed—even if they have not been successful in math in the past. One of her refrains is "Everybody here is brilliant," and she talks about expectations every day, all year long. She also connects learning goals to students' life goals. A project about financial planning, for example, is readily applicable for college-bound students.

Many of Norfar's students will be the first in their families to attend college. "That means there's no one in their family who knows how it all works," she says. "Even though we're helping another family with financial planning for the project, I am also helping my students understand college planning."

Similarly, humanities teacher Erin Brandvold looks for opportunities to "just be super-positive." For example, if a student asks her which reading choice is the easiest, she will reply, "It's the one you're most interested in. That's what will keep you going."

Another belief shared by most Project Based Teachers is that students deserve to know the purpose for what they are learning. PBL makes that "why" obvious by connecting academic concepts to real-world contexts. Well-designed projects naturally answer the perennial student question "When will we ever need to know this?" Making sure students have an authentic audience for their efforts is another way that teachers bring meaning to learning experiences.

For chemistry teacher Ray Ahmed, the goal with PBL "is to strategically help students learn core academic content around things they care about." At the same time, he cares about meeting students' social and emotional needs. "That's where projects come in nicely," he says. "You can address all the aspects of social and emotional *and* intellectual learning through a project that engages the students."

Although these veteran teachers want PBL to be engaging for students, they also recognize that this approach to learning is not easy. In words and actions, Project Based Teachers convey their belief that students can rise to the challenge and produce high-quality work to meet demanding goals.

Norfar's students have been known to say, "Why don't you just tell us the answer?" Her response reflects her beliefs and values: "I honor what students say. I listen if they need to vent. But then I tell them, 'You need to grow. If you only learn by someone telling you, you're going to have a hard time when you have to figure things out for yourself. I'll scaffold it for you so you can succeed. You may have to wrestle. There's nothing wrong with being stuck. Just breathe, and then approach it in a different way.'"

In her comments, we can hear the core values and beliefs that are shared by effective PBL teachers—and that are critical to building a positive culture for learning.

Shared Norms: Creating a Community of Project Based Learners

Visit a PBL classroom and you are likely to see banners, posters, or slogans that convey class norms. These typically sound different from rules, which tend to be teacher-generated and are often heavy on "dos and don'ts" (e.g., "Get to class on time"; "Don't use profanity"). Rules are about enforcement and control. Norms, on the other hand, are shared agreements about how classmates and teachers treat one another and what they value as a community of learners. In PBL, shared norms support a learning culture that is inclusive, respectful, and fair (see Figure 1.1).

Coming to a consensus about norms builds a strong foundation for PBL. Taking part in norm setting tells students that they have a voice in how the classroom operates. When they work to uphold those norms, they hold everyone accountable, including themselves, their peers, and the teacher. This process shifts the traditional power dynamic and fosters a more democratic classroom.

Students bring a wide range of cultural norms, expectations, and practices from their home environments. Educators, too, bring their own assumptions and biases. The goal of creating shared norms is to promote a classroom culture that values what each person brings while establishing common expectations for the group.

Figure 1.1   Culture Builders

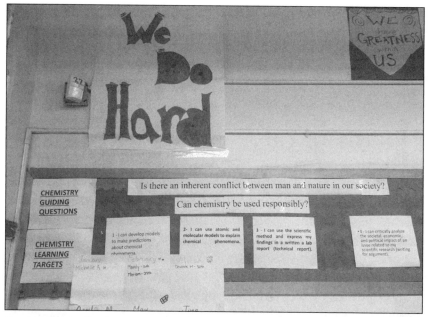

Shared norms and positive slogans are prominently featured in Ray Ahmed's classroom. (Photo used with permission from John Larmer.)

Let's take a look at the norms adopted by Norfar's high school math classes in Figure 1.2 (p. 21), which reinforce a culture of "fair and engaging learning." You'll notice that these statements are worded clearly and positively for both teacher ("Help students understand") and students ("Advocate for yourself"), with the stated goal of creating a fair and engaging learning environment. Everyone had a voice in creating the norms, and everyone is accountable for enforcing them.

Teachers go about establishing norms in different ways, depending on students' age and developmental level, their previous experience with norms, and the broader school culture. Practical considerations also come into play. Norfar, for example, teaches several preps each day. Early in the school year, she introduces a mini-project that poses this driving question: *How can we create a fair and engaging learning environment for math?* Students in every class period contribute to the brainstorming about shared norms and vote to reach a consensus. Norfar then synthesizes that input to arrive at one set of norms for all classes (as captured in Figure 1.2), including expectations for students and the teacher.

Visit Sherry Griesinger's classroom in Novi, Michigan, and you'll see a poster of norms that were obviously generated by her community of 2nd graders. They include agreements such as

- Keep everyone happy.
- Make smart choices.
- Take care of our stuff and each other.
- Follow directions quickly.

The students and teacher then use hand signals and simple gestures to reinforce their norms. For example, a tap at the temple might mean "I'm making a smart choice."

Even the youngest learners are ready to establish norms together. With her 5-year-old transitional kindergarten students, teacher Sara Lev starts the school year by asking, "How should we treat each other? What are our hopes for the year?" Students learn immediately that their voice matters. "It's so different than if I came in and laid down the rules," Lev says. "I'm constantly asking students what they think."

Ray Ahmed starts building a positive classroom culture with his chemistry students right off the bat: "The first days are all about building culture and managing activities that students do in class. If you pick the right activity, you bring to life the norms you're trying to set." From day one, he has students working on learning activities in small groups. He sits in on their discussions in the role of coach and conferences with students individually about their progress. He introduces protocols such as gallery walks for peer critique. "Right away, there's a lot of talking, thinking, and working together. I'm doing a lot of reinforcing of positive behaviors. That's different than saying you can't do this or that."

Figure 1.2   Shared Norms

Teacher and Student Norms	
Below are the norms for the teacher(s) and students. Norms are what we agree to do as a class to make this a fair and engaging learning environment. We will check in on the norms each week.	
Teacher Norms	**Student Norms**

1. Teach in different ways.
2. Call students by their names.
3. Care about students' feelings.
   a. Understand their situation
4. Have a good attitude.
   a. Stay calm.
   b. Use kind words.
   c. Have patience.
   d. Greet students and say good-bye.
5. Help students understand.
   a. Work at a reasonable pace.
   b. Explain clearly.
   c. Support different learning styles.
   d. Expect the best.
   e. Re-explain if necessary.
6. Attend school the majority of the time.
7. Be respectful.
   a. Give everyone what they need.
   b. Use proper language.
   c. Allow space if needed.
   d. Use supportive words when explaining.
   e. Call by your name.
8. Have a growth mindset.
	1. Have a growth mindset.
	   a. Believe you can improve.
	   b. Fail forward.
	   c. Keep trying.
	   d. Speak positively about your abilities
	     to learn.
	2. Call classmates by their names.
	3. Be responsible for your work.
	   a. Have materials ready.
	   b. Advocate for yourself.
	   c. Be a professional.
	   d. Meet deadlines.
	   e. Participate.
	   f. Be on time to class.
	4. Listen…
	   a. to the teacher.
	   b. to your classmates.
	   c. to guests.
	   d. to the directions.
	5. Attend school the majority of the time.
	6. Be a good team player.
	   a. Provide good, helpful feedback.
	   b. Stay calm.
	   c. Encourage others.
	   d. Stay on topic.
	   e. Be considerate.
	   f. Use proper language.
	   g. Communicate clearly to students and
	     teacher(s).

Teacher and students commit to these agreements in Telannia Norfar's math classes.

Some teachers build their class norms by building on a foundation of schoolwide agreements. While not every school has established schoolwide agreements, these are increasingly common in schools that have adopted programs such as Positive Behavioral Interventions and Supports (www.pbis.org) and Responsive Classroom (www.responsiveclassroom.org).

Abby Schneiderjohn is a 4th grade teacher in San Jose, California. She joined Steindorf STEAM Elementary School just as the public magnet school was opening its doors in 2016. Steindorf has adopted Positive Behavioral Interventions and Supports as a schoolwide framework. As part of the overarching school culture, students (and adults) at all grade levels share these three expectations: "We are caring and respectful. We are responsible decision makers. We are problem solvers."

Schneiderjohn started with those broad statements and then asked her students to define—in their own words—how these norms would play out in their classroom. Writing class expectations together was a collaborative experience, but that was just the start of building the culture. The real value comes from reinforcing norms over time. "As new situations come up, we go back to our norms. For example, when we got a class set of Chromebooks, we talked about how we were going to use them effectively. What's the appropriate use?" Class norms provide both students and teachers with a set of guiding principles for learning together.

◆ Try This: "T" Up Class Norms

Here's how Todd Finley (2014), education blogger and professor of English education at East Carolina University, breaks down his process for engaging students in norming:

1. Start by explaining why norms are important for learning (share the "why").

2. Then have students work in small groups to generate T-charts. The left column asks them to describe a specific example of something that has interfered with their learning. (For example: *When students laugh at kids who make a mistake, we are reluctant to participate in a class discussion.*) In the right column, teams suggest a norm to prevent that problem from happening. (For example: *We learn from mistakes.*)

3. As a whole-class activity, list everyone's proposed norms and facilitate a discussion. Which ones help build trust and respect, encourage inquiry, and promote effort to produce good results? What's missing?

4. Finally, have students vote on which norms to adopt. Share their final list as a classroom artifact, perhaps as a student-made poster that everyone signs.

5. Continue to refer to these norms throughout the year, and encourage students to reinforce them with their peers.

Physical Environment: The Right Stuff Matters

The physical environment for PBL sends clues and signals about the classroom culture. Some clues are as obvious as wheels on chairs to encourage flexible seating. (If your school hasn't invested in flexible furnishings, you can "hack" your way to a low-cost version by putting tennis balls on chair legs to make them slide quietly and easily.) Other clues send more subtle messages about who "owns" the space. Are there writable surfaces—such as poster paper, whiteboards, or even windows—for capturing student brainstorming? Are students empowered to use technology as needed during projects, or do tech tools stay primarily under teacher control? Putting tools into students' hands promotes student voice and choice, and it reinforces the partnership between teacher and learners.

Abby Schneiderjohn's elementary classroom is designed to maximize flexibility. Chairs are on wheels, and desks are trapezoids that can be configured as rectangles of four, circles of six, or semicircles of three. "It's all super-flexible," she says, which allows for fast rearrangements necessitated by different learning activities during projects.

That doesn't mean students are playing bumper cars. Schneiderjohn is deliberate and transparent about matching the physical setup of the classroom to the learning activity at hand. When a project calls for collaboration, students sit in teams. When students need individual think time, she signals them to "unzip" and make some space between desks. She's considerate, too, of students who need more structure. "It can be overwhelming for some if we switch it up too often."

While flexible furnishings such as this can be an advantage, they aren't essential for PBL. More important is the message about how the space supports student-driven learning.

Elementary teacher Erin Gannon suggests engaging students in the classroom setup as a culture-building activity. "Let them decide the needs of the space for them to be successful. If they create workspaces that allow for collaboration, and they decide where they'll sit, that sets a powerful stage at the start of the year."

A PBL-friendly environment also makes supports and scaffolds for student learning visible and accessible. We will discuss strategies to scaffold student learning in Chapter 5, but here are three physical artifacts to consider as culture builders.

Project wall: By dedicating a bulletin board or other prominent display space to the project currently underway, you create a central location to manage information, highlight upcoming deadlines and milestones, remind students of the driving question, capture need-to-knows, and point to resources (see Figure 1.3). Although a project wall might sound like an ideal tool for focusing the attention of young learners, it's equally effective with older students. Instructional coach Ian Stevenson uses a project wall as a teaching tool with high school students. Rather than a static display, their wall is a dynamic space where students post new research questions, use rubrics to assess their learning, and manage their team and individual progress. A digital space can serve the same purpose if all students have ready access to technology.

Figure 1.3 Project Wall

In an elementary classroom, questions and resources guide student learning in a language arts project. (Photo used with permission from John Larmer.)

Sentence starters: Student voice and choice are essential elements for high-quality PBL, but not every student may be comfortable sharing his or her thoughts aloud. For a variety of reasons, some students will need more processing time or support to take part in active discussions. Sentence starters can help get discussions flowing. For example, these sentence starters encourage argumentation and critical thinking: "I see it another way because..." or "Have you thought about...?" or "Here's the evidence that supports my conclusion ..." For English language learners, sentence starters reinforce a culture of safety and trust; students know how to engage with one another productively and appropriately.

Evidence of the "messy middle": PBL is often described—lovingly—as messy learning. Don't hide the productive mess that comes with making prototypes and rough drafts. Instead, keep it visible. Use students' works-in-process as opportunities to ask questions, make observations, and provide formative feedback. There will be plenty of time later to showcase their final, polished products.

❯ Try This: Classroom Audit

Take a classroom audit of your physical environment to look for evidence of a positive culture for learning. What do you notice when you take stock of the following?

- **What students see:** How well do photos, posters, and other pieces of artwork reflect students' cultures and diverse backgrounds? Are you building a culture that's welcoming to all? Do students have a choice about what's on display? Were the artifacts purchased by the teacher or school, or were they made or contributed by students?

- **What students are thinking and saying:** Are students' ideas captured in their own words on whiteboards or displays of shared norms? Is there any evidence of student work in progress or only final, polished products on display? Do you see sentence frames or word walls to support language learning and scaffold academic conversations?

- **Seating arrangements:** How flexible is your classroom setup? Can students easily change seating arrangements for different learning activities (i.e., individual, pairs, small groups)? Does furniture accommodate special needs, such as "wobble" stools that allow for fidgeting?

- **Who "owns" the stuff:** How accessible are the tools, books, and other resources students need for learning (including technology)?

- **Learning in process:** Can you tell at a glance what sort of project this community of learners is working on? Are there signals that the shared goal is high-quality work? For example, do you see rubrics or other criteria for excellence? Are there exemplars of high-quality work available for students to use as models for their own work?

Based on your audit, consider changes in the physical environment you want to make to improve the classroom culture. To promote inclusivity, how might you involve students or their families in the process?

Protocols and Routines: Habits for a Student-Centered Classroom

Protocols and routines are commonplace in education—and for good reason. Familiar procedures increase efficiency and improve classroom management, preserving time and attention for the business of learning. Through repetition, routines become automatic, requiring little instruction or oversight from the teacher (Lemov, 2015). For example, teachers often have routines for how students turn in homework or how they pass out materials.

Protocols are structured processes that encourage active listening and reflection while keeping a conversation focused on a specific topic or problem. Used effectively, protocols ensure that all voices in a group are heard and valued (Mattoon, 2015). That makes them useful for building a collaborative culture.

In PBL, it's important to adopt routines that reinforce the culture of student-centered learning. If you don't want the teacher to be the class expert in all things, then encourage students to turn to one another as information sources with the routine "Ask three before me."

When students are new to PBL, they may question why school "feels different." That's a fair question that goes to the heart of classroom culture, and it deserves a thoughtful response. One PBL veteran makes a point of helping each new class of 4th graders unlearn routines that emphasize compliance and passivity (e.g., raising hands and sitting quietly until called upon). He encourages a more conversational classroom where students talk and learn together as they engage in projects. That doesn't mean he invites chaos. With simple hand signals, he helps students recognize when they need to moderate the noise level or transition from teamwork to a whole-class activity.

Like routines, protocols matter in PBL. By using protocols such as gallery walks to focus their feedback, students learn how to give and receive criticism and how to use feedback to make their own work better in subsequent drafts.

❍ Try This: Hold a Gallery Walk

A gallery walk is a critique protocol in which students get feedback from their peers on how to improve their work. Schedule a gallery walk at one or more points during a project as part of your formative assessment plan. (A word of caution: In advance of doing any critique protocol, make sure that students understand how to give and receive critical feedback. Consider modeling the process or using role-plays, sentence starters, and other activities to build and reinforce a positive critique culture.) Here are the basic steps for a gallery walk:

1. Post work to be assessed on classroom walls (or display it digitally). This may be text, storyboards, prototypes of products, or other artifacts.

2. Decide on the process for giving feedback. Students can write on sticky notes to be placed next to the work displayed, write on a feedback form posted next to the work, or use a digital tool to write comments and questions.

3. Be sure students know what to look for. Explain the criteria to be applied, or have them use a rubric or checklist for guidance. Suggest sentence starters to frame their feedback (e.g., "I like," "I wish," "I wonder").

4. Have students move around the room (or go through a digital display) *silently* to give feedback, allowing enough time to assess each piece of work displayed.

5. After the gallery walk, ask the person or team that created the work to read and reflect on the feedback they got. Then plan next steps/revisions.

Time Needed: Approximately 20–30 minutes, depending on how much work is displayed, how complex the assessment is, and how much time is allotted for Step 5.

Variations:

- If the work requires an explanation before other students can offer feedback, have one member of the team that created it stay with the work instead of moving around the room.

- The students who created the work to be assessed may post a question or two about which they would especially like feedback. For example, "Does our product sound like it would appeal to our target audience?" or "Did we include convincing evidence?"

Information about other critique protocols, such as the Charrette and the Tuning Protocol, can be found at www.bie.org.

In addition to gallery walks, PBL veterans leverage a variety of protocols and routines that build and reinforce a positive classroom culture. Try your hand at these ideas (many of which you will hear more about in coming chapters).

Morning meetings: These are regularly scheduled, low-risk opportunities to check in with students at the start of class. Morning meetings (sometimes called circles) are helpful for building community, strengthening relationships, amplifying student voice, and supporting students' social and emotional learning. (Learn more about structures for morning meetings from Responsive Classroom: www.responsiveclassroom.org/what-is-morning-meeting.)

Thinking routines: Thinking routines, such as "think, pair, share" or "see, think, wonder," develop habits of mind important in PBL, such as curiosity, along with content understanding. (Find more examples at Harvard's Project Zero: www.visiblethinkingpz.org.)

Fishbowl: A fishbowl is a discussion protocol that can be used for modeling, discussions, or peer feedback. A small group inside the fishbowl actively participates while a larger group listens and observes from an outer circle. Students can then swap positions so that everyone eventually has a role as both participant and observer. (Learn more from Facing History and Ourselves: www.facinghistory.org/resource-library/teaching-strategies/fishbowl.)

Closers: End-of-class routines provide opportunities to bring everyone together to focus on the accomplishments and challenges of the day and reinforce shared norms. During projects, students are often working on different learning activities or with small teams for most of class. Closing routines bring everyone back together, even if briefly, to reconnect as a learning community and anticipate what will happen next in the project. Teacher Erin Brandvold closes each class period by saying, "You're brilliant. Hardworking. Perseverant."

Reflections: Reflection prompts and protocols invite students to think about their own learning. When used consistently, reflection becomes a habit of mind. Not surprisingly, reflection is an essential element of Gold Standard PBL.

Celebrations: Celebrations of learning shouldn't wait until the end of projects. High-fives, shout-outs, fist bumps, and other simple routines celebrate the small but important accomplishments that unfold along the way.

When introducing protocols that are new to students, take time to explain their purpose. For example, a gallery walk gives students a chance to see other students' works-in-progress and offer constructive feedback to inform the next draft. Consider using a role-play or fishbowl to model how a protocol works. Introduce sentence stems to keep the protocol focused. Encourage students to compare and contrast effective responses with responses that are not so helpful.

To emphasize the authenticity of PBL, help students see that the skills they are developing through the use of protocols—such as being able to give and receive critical feedback or understand others' perspectives—are important not only in school but also in contexts outside the classroom.

Start Small to Start Strong

Starting a new semester or school year with a mini-project is a smart move that helps students get accustomed to the processes and flow of PBL. Instead of starting the school year with reading assignments or labs, high school science teacher Brandon Cohen begins with a mini-project in which students create their own infographic résumés. This starter project makes sense for several reasons. It helps the teacher build strong relationships with students by having them identify their skills, strengths, and interests. Then "later in the semester, when we get into the hard science and more rigorous projects," Cohen says, "we've already developed that trust."

The infographics project also allows Cohen to introduce software tools and teach students to convey information graphically. He knows that students will need those skills later in the course, when they make signs to explain their scientific products to public audiences. Equally important, the short-term project enables the teacher to introduce students to protocols for critique and revision that they will continue using throughout the semester. "This helps to develop the structures of our class," he explains. Students learn early in the year how to give and receive criticism and how to use feedback to make their work better in subsequent drafts.

Relatively short, small-scale, low-risk starter projects "let you go heavy on the cultural elements," says PBL veteran Feroze Munshi. Like Cohen, Munshi invests time early to teach students how to give and receive critical feedback. He fosters a culture of craftsmanship by encouraging students to reflect on the satisfaction of producing high-quality work. "These are complicated skills that take time to develop," he adds. "It's my job help students acclimate to the PBL culture." If you build that culture early, students will be ready to tackle longer, more content-heavy projects later in the school year.

Abby Schneiderjohn also uses a starter project as a culture builder with her 4th graders. Although their STEAM magnet school is relatively young, it is housed in an older building. Some students know one another from previous schools, whereas others are getting acquainted for the first time. "I want us to come together as a community from day one," she says. "I want students to go home that day excited about school." As an entry event, she has construction workers show her students a time capsule they unearthed during renovations. That sets the stage for their driving question: *What makes me a unique member of my community?* "From there," Schneiderjohn says, "students launch into learning the history of the school and of themselves."

During the time capsule project, students take part in daily investigations, team-building activities, and personal reflections. "These are all activities that teachers would naturally do at the beginning of the school year," Schneiderjohn says, "but we do them in the context of the project. That makes everything flow so much smoother."

For their final product, students use the school's makerspace to create artifacts for their time capsule that reflect something about themselves. Then they present their products to parents at an exhibition. Parents give them feedback, using the same sentence stems that students had learned to use for critique ("I like," "I wish," "What if?"). Through this short-term experience, both students and parents are fully immersed in the PBL culture. "It's a great way to jump in," Schneiderjohn says.

Schneiderjohn's example underscores the importance of investing time and intention in building the PBL culture. Everyone involved in the learning community needs to feel welcome and included in creating and supporting a positive culture. That means parents as well as teachers and students. Use opportunities to connect with parents—such as back-to-school nights, conferences, and class newsletters or web pages—to help families understand why PBL may look and feel different from more traditional school.

Here are two more ideas for mini-projects to help you and your students get off to a fast start:

Cracking the Case: When Julia Cagle and Tom Lee were teaching in a freshmen academy at Morris Innovative High School in Dalton, Georgia, they started the school year with high drama. Students arrived on campus the first week of school to find a mystery that needed to be solved. To crack the case, students had to generate questions, consider evidence, and team up with classmates to compare conclusions. There was no point in sitting and waiting for instructions—they had to get active if they were going to figure out whodunit. Meanwhile, teachers had the opportunity to get acquainted with students and watch their interactions with one another. "This was a cool way to get calibrated to Project Based Learning," says Eric White, who was previously an instructional coach at the school. "An induction project like this starts things off with a bang and builds a culture of teamwork. It's worth the time up front to introduce students to PBL processes."

Lip Dub: At Applied Technology Center, a PBL high school in Montebello, California, students spent their first two days of the school year working on a "lip dub" music video production to celebrate their school. Teacher Krystal Diaz credits the school's student leaders with planning and organizing the event. Students embraced the lip dub as a way to build school pride while giving incoming 9th graders a crash course in PBL processes. The mini-project was intentionally light on academic content but heavy on culture. Within two days, students had to go from team building and brainstorming to filming and editing. Mistakes offered opportunities for do-overs, reinforcing a culture of risk taking and learning from failures. To help adults facilitate this collaborative experience, student leaders produced a time line and facilitation guide. The mini-project was structured so that every student had an assigned role, which played to his or her strengths. Although students and teachers took the work seriously, they didn't forget the fun factor. Says Diaz, "Our lip dub gave us the chance to become closer as a school, a chance to make something together, and a chance to build a culture—a PBL culture."

> ### ❂ Try This: Build Team Spirit
>
> Team-building activities are shorter than starter projects but offer big benefits when it comes to building a collaborative culture for PBL. Elementary teacher Jim Bentley likes to use team builders like rope challenges or the popular Marshmallow Challenge outside academic content so that collaboration skills are the main focus. Coming up with a team name or logo can also be an effective team-building activity. Middle school teacher Heather Wolpert-Gawron kicked off a new school year by having student teams solve clues to open a "breakout box" she left on each table. "Each lock can only be opened by working together to solve a clue," she explained. Along with cracking clues, student teams had to work together to solve puzzles that related to content. (Learn more about breakout boxes for education at www.breakoutedu.com. For more team-building activities, see the creative practice problems at Odyssey of the Mind—www.odysseyofthemind.com—or the quick games to get groups working well together at Gamestorming, http://gamestorming.com/category/games-for-opening.)
>
> After any team builder, take time to have students debrief: What helped or hindered their team's effort? Did everyone on the team have a voice and chance to contribute their talents? If they could do the challenge again, what would they want to do differently?

Coaches' Notebook: Culture Builders

If you have access to an instructional coach in your school system, take advantage of this resource to support your growth in PBL. For example, invite the coach to visit your classroom. What does he or she see and hear that indicates a culture that is welcoming, is respectful of students' home cultures, and invites student voice and choice? What's missing? An instructional coach or other colleague who is versed in PBL can bring an extra set of eyes and ears to help you fine-tune your practice.

To help teachers build a classroom culture that fosters student thinking and supports PBL, instructional coach Myla Lee uses informal observations, structured protocols, and evidence to encourage productive coaching conversations. Among the tools in her coaching toolkit are the following techniques.

Ghost walk: This protocol is among those recommended by Ron Ritchhart, Harvard professor and author of *Creating Cultures of Thinking* (2015). It starts with the teacher generating a list of what he or she would expect to see as evidence of a culture of thinking. With that list in hand, Lee walks through the classroom when there are no students present. She takes photos and makes notes. Then she debriefs with the teacher about the evidence she has gathered. For example, how much of the "stuff" on the walls was made by students? Does it tell the story of learning in progress, or is it only the final, polished product? How well do the artifacts reflect students' home cultures? Are there mixed or confusing messages?

Data collection: In response to teacher request, Lee will do a brief data collection during class time. "Teachers may want to know more about student questioning, so I will spend 30 minutes in class tallying what I hear. Who's asking the questions? What kinds of questions do students ask? Then I'll have a coaching conversation with the teacher. I'll share the data and ask, 'What do you notice?' That often gets them to an aha. They'll say, 'Wow, I did all the talking! I asked all the questions!'"

Informal observations: Informal classroom visits give Lee more information to bring into coaching conversations with teachers. The more specific her observations can be, the better. For example, are students using protocols and thinking routines during traditional lessons that could also be useful in PBL? Does the teacher make scaffolds readily available to support language learners and reinforce academic vocabulary? Are students working well in groups, or do they need to learn new routines to support collaboration before teaming up on a project?

When it comes to classroom culture, Lee adds, it's worth remembering that PBL is not just what happens in one unit. "It's a culture that takes shape long before the project begins. When that culture is in place, you see it and feel it."

Not every teacher has access to instructional coaching. If this support is not provided in your school setting, think about inviting peer teachers, grade-level or content-area leaders, or administrators to provide focused feedback to help you fine-tune your PBL practice.

Strategies to Build the Culture: Key Takeaways

In this chapter, you have read about a number of strategies to help you build a positive classroom culture that will support all learners in PBL. Which of these strategies are already part of your practice? Which strategies are you ready to introduce next?

Beliefs and values: What do you do and say to encourage

- High expectations for all? How do you let students know you think they can succeed (and will support them through challenges)?
- A culture of excellence? How do you encourage students to aim for high-quality work and not simply check off assignments?
- A growth mindset? How do you communicate and model the need to put in effort to get results?
- A welcoming and safe community? How do you help every student feel included and valued?

Shared norms: Do students have a voice in establishing and reinforcing norms for learning together? How do you use shared norms not only to kick off the year but also to sustain a positive culture for the long term?

Physical environment: How might you increase the flexibility of your physical space to allow students to work independently, in small groups, or as a whole class? Do students have ready access to the tools and resources they need during PBL? What's on their wish list?

Routines and protocols: Which of the many routines and protocols mentioned in this chapter are already part of your teaching practice? How are you incorporating them into PBL?

On Your PBL Bookshelf

Creating Cultures of Thinking: The 8 Forces We Must Master to Truly Transform Our Schools: Ron Ritchhart, senior research associate with Project Zero at the Harvard Graduate School of Education, dives deeply into thinking about thinking in this practical book. With classroom vignettes and probing questions, he prompts teachers to closely examine everything from the language they use to the routines they introduce to encourage student voice, inquiry, and other nonnegotiables for PBL.

Culturally Responsive Teaching and the Brain: Promoting Authentic Engagement and Rigor Among Culturally and Linguistically Diverse Students: Author and educator Zaretta L. Hammond connects insights from neuroscience with strategies for culturally responsive instruction. Her strategies for closing the achievement gap begin with the belief that all children can think critically and learn deeply.

An Ethic of Excellence: Building a Culture of Craftsmanship with Students: Ron Berger, chief program officer for EL Schools (and well known among PBLers as the star of the *Austin's Butterfly* video), makes a compelling case for attending to craftsmanship and quality.

Identity Safe Classrooms: Places to Belong and Learn: Veteran educators Dorothy M. Steele and Becki Cohn-Vargas use the term *identity safe classroom* to describe learning environments where every child feels welcome and eager to learn, especially those who have previously experienced repeated failure, heavy-handed discipline, or negative stereotypes. The authors encourage setting high expectations for all learners, cultivating diversity as a resource, and encouraging students to make choices and take responsibility for their learning.

School Climate Change: How Do I Build a Positive Environment for Learning? This short-format book by Peter DeWitt and Sean Slade offers practical strategies to promote equity and create a safe, welcoming school climate.

2
Design and Plan

*Intentional design of the learning experience sets the stage
for students and teachers to capitalize on the full potential of PBL.*

When middle school teacher Kimberly Head-Trotter designs projects for 6th grade English language arts and social studies, she says, "I'm looking for a way to make the learning relatable for my students. If it's relatable, I know that students will take ownership." Experience has taught her that connecting projects to students' lives and to their community helps them better understand the purpose of learning.

Of course, Head-Trotter also keeps in mind the content standards she needs to meet. "That's what we have to teach," she says matter-of-factly. Before getting too narrowly focused on establishing learning goals and aligning to standards, though, Head-Trotter tunes into the interests of her Nashville, Tennessee, students. She knows from previous conversations, for example, that her students at McKissack Middle School are curious about the history of the civil rights movement. Their grandparents may have been witnesses—or even participants—in important events that took place in Nashville, giving students a personal connection to history. "That interest is going to sustain them over a project," Head-Trotter says.

In this chapter, we'll see how she went from the spark of an idea about the civil rights movement to an academically rigorous project that had a strong local focus. The backstory of her project will highlight effective strategies you can use to design and plan high-quality PBL experiences for your students.

Getting Started

When teachers are new to PBL, they often ask if project design should start with content standards or if it's better to begin with a compelling idea that's certain to engage students. Figuring out which comes first can feel a bit like a chicken-and-egg question. The answer is often "a little of both."

Let's start by considering where to find promising project ideas. From there, we'll describe the design process that will take you from inspiration to implementation by paying close attention to Essential Project Design Elements.

As you'll see in the examples that follow, project planning gets better with feedback, reflection, and revision—the same practices that help students produce high-quality work during projects.

> ■ A companion video about designing and planning a project can be found at www.bie.org.

Where to Find Good Project Ideas

Just as PBL allows for student voice and choice, project planning is an invitation for teachers to make choices and get creative. Designing a project is an opportunity for you to be the architect of your students' learning experience. To inspire your thinking, consider a wide range of sources for project-worthy ideas. Here are some strategies that have inspired other teachers.

Borrow and adapt: Perhaps the fastest way to get started with PBL planning is to borrow an idea from another teacher or program and adapt it to fit your classroom context. The Buck Institute for Education (BIE) maintains an extensive project library just for this purpose. It's searchable by grade level and subject area. (Visit the project library at www.bie.org.) Many curriculum providers also produce ready-made project plans. Review these with a critical eye to make sure they contain all the elements of Gold Standard PBL (as described on pages 47–48; see also Figure 2.1 on page 49). To see examples of PBL in action, explore the BIE video collection (www.bie.org) or find more PBL videos at www.edutopia.org.

For 4th grade teacher Meghan Ashkanani from Novi, Michigan, being able to borrow and adapt an existing idea from the BIE library gave her a jump start on her first project. She recalls, "When I realized that there are examples you can tweak, I remember thinking, 'Thank goodness!'" She was motivated to try PBL because she saw the advantages for her students but admits, "I worried about doing it wrong. I wasn't sure how to create everything from scratch. That felt overwhelming. To see examples that fit with what we know we need to teach—that was a big advantage." In particular, she was attracted to a project example in which students presented their inventions "Shark Tank"–style. "I could see how the pieces fit together. On my own, I might not have been that creative."

Remodel: Take a fresh look at units you have taught in the past and see how you might remodel them as Project Based Learning. A benefit of this approach is that you already know the content well. You also have a good sense of student interest in (or, perhaps, lack of engagement with) the topic. If your traditional unit has left students asking the dreaded "When will we ever need to know this?" question, then maybe it's time to remodel it into a project that emphasizes real-world connections.

Meghan Ashkanani had traditionally taught persuasive writing by having her 4th graders write a letter to their parents making a case for why they should get a puppy. It was a cute assignment, and parents seemed to enjoy receiving the letters, but the lesson did not produce terribly meaningful outcomes. Nobody ever got a puppy!

As she became more comfortable with PBL, Ashkanani recognized the opportunity to remodel the lesson into a more authentic project. The spark was a current events discussion about how the video game Minecraft was being used in education. Minecraft is a game many students enjoy playing during their out-of-school time, and they all agreed that it would be cool if they could bring the game into the school day.

With that inspiration and her prior experience of building on existing PBL plans, Ashkanani was ready to design a new project that was focused on the learning goal of persuasive writing. However, this time around, students would be writing to (and speaking with) a more public audience of decision makers. Their driving question was *How can we persuade our PTO to purchase a school license for Minecraft: Education Edition?* Students made such a convincing case, backed by research, that their persuasive arguments got the desired results.

Listen: Student questions offer a renewable source of project inspiration. The key is to deliberately listen for what interests, inspires, or provokes students and then look for connections to your learning goals. What do students bring up during morning meetings or in informal conversations? During class discussions, do you hear questions that indicate a desire to go deeper with a topic?

Earlier in his teaching career, Ray Ahmed used to puzzle over this question: "How do we engage kids into caring about things that adults care about?" With more experience, he realized that he had been asking the wrong question. "We should be asking, 'How do we get students engaged [academically] around things that they do care about?'" That shift in thinking has helped him design chemistry projects that arise from students' communities, concerns, and interests. "I used to sit for weeks during the summer trying to come up with project ideas. Kids come up with so many better projects than I can."

If you're not hearing students ask interesting questions, you might want to prompt their thinking by surveying them about their interests or have them interview one another. Some teachers reserve space on a whiteboard or wall to capture interesting student questions that may eventually lead to projects.

In Rhode Island, 3rd grade teachers Lorie Loughborough and Linda Spinney were leading a fairly traditional lesson about their state symbols when a student asked, "Why don't we have a state insect?" That question was the spark for a project in which students advocated to have the endangered American burying beetle designated as their official state insect. Instead of learning only superficially about state symbols, students dove deeply into an investigation of habitats, endangered species, and government. They got real results, convincing the state legislature to pass a law designating their favorite beetle as the state insect.

Similarly, high school teacher Mike Gwaltney encouraged his students to learn about government by actively participating in civic affairs. Students chose issues they wanted to influence and then planned actions that would use the levers of government to effect change. One team, for example, argued before the city council—and, eventually, before the state legislature—in support of a local gun control measure to increase public safety near schools. "I didn't want students to just read about citizenship," Gwaltney explains. "I wanted them to *be citizens.*"

Teach from the headlines: What's happening in your community or the wider world that has your students buzzing? How do these events connect to your content? Instead of stopping at a brief current events discussion, consider designing a project that has a "ripped-from-the-headlines" feel.

Dara Laws Savage teaches English at Early College High School at Delaware State University. When a controversy surfaced over racial discrimination in the Academy Awards nominations (summarized by the hashtag #OscarsSoWhite), she knew she had found a news hook for an engaging project. She created the Carter Awards as a project to honor historian Carter G. Woodson, who is credited with founding Black History Month. Savage challenged her students to produce their own nomination packets, modeled on the Oscars, using writing, video clips, and critical thinking to support nominations in several categories of accomplishments.

Connect projects to popular culture: Which books are your students reading for pleasure? Which movies or recording artists are current favorites? Connecting projects to students' cultural interests is a well-tested route to engagement. Teachers have leveraged popular works such as *The Hunger Games,* for example, to design projects that focus on the rise of totalitarianism and conflicts in world history.

Respond to real requests: Perhaps your students could address a real need identified by a partner or collaborator. Their "client" might be a nonprofit organization, local government agency, business, or even a teacher or classroom in another grade level.

Jim Bentley teaches upper elementary students in Elk Grove, California. Several years ago, he began using digital storytelling projects to teach across the curriculum. His students have become so adept at making documentaries and instructional films that they now receive requests from the community to produce short films and public-service announcements. (Read more about how he manages these content-rich projects in Chapter 4.)

High school students at Iowa BIG in Des Moines, Iowa, routinely team up with local partners on projects that leverage student interests, community problem solving, and academic content. As a result of these authentic partnerships, students have created a dance therapy curriculum to promote inclusion for people with special needs, investigated the use of drones for agriculture, and engineered a plan to redevelop an abandoned meatpacking property for recreational use.

Build on your passions: Tuning in to student interests is one good source of project ideas, but don't overlook your own passions as another wellspring of PBL inspiration.

Middle school teacher and blogger Heather Wolpert-Gawron (2014) shares this PBL design tip: "I want to be excited about what I'm about to present to the kids.... Design towards what you love... and the interests of the age group you teach" (paras. 6, 20). She often starts with an idea that she finds inherently interesting, such as the science of superheroes, and then looks for connections to content standards.

Similarly, high school teacher Mike Kaechele designed an ambitious interdisciplinary project about the future of his hometown of Grand Rapids, Michigan, after getting interested in citizen-led efforts to restore the city's namesake river rapids. It wasn't an issue that his students were even aware of until he immersed them in a locally relevant project that incorporated history, environmental science, and language arts.

Codesign with students: Starting with the problems or challenges your students want to tackle, work with them to codesign projects that incorporate academic learning goals. This is how high school teacher Ray Ahmed designs second-semester chemistry projects that are meaningful to students and also aligned to high-stakes graduation standards. During the first semester, when he is introducing students to PBL processes, he takes more of the lead on project design. "Early in the year, I tip the scale in my favor in terms of who's asking the big questions," he says. But by the second semester, "kids are ready to ask the questions themselves. They have the idea, they implement it, and they defend what they found in front of a panel of experts." Among their recent projects: how to clean up a local oil spill with nontoxic dispersants, how to keep makeup from oxidizing, and how to choose which pesticide to use to control an algae bloom in a local lake. With students driving the learning, Ahmed sees his role as incorporating chemistry content into their projects. "I know the content. It's my job to make sure that the applicable content is in their projects."

Join an Existing Project

Instead of going it alone with your first PBL effort, consider the advantages of joining an existing project. This allows you to start with plans that have already been developed and then fine-tune them to meet your context. You'll also gain access to one or more collaborators who can share wisdom when it comes to project implementation.

You can join ongoing projects at the following sites:

- **e-NABLE** (www.enablingthefuture.org): This is a community of educators and STEM advocates who are guiding students to use 3D printers for humanitarian purposes. Students have designed and built prosthetic hands for children who need them, using the e-NABLE platform to connect student designers with recipients who need the devices. The site includes resources to support learning for students and teachers alike.
- **iEARN** (International Education and Resource Network, www. iearn.org): This is a nonprofit network that engages students and teachers from 140 countries in collaborative projects. Teachers can join existing projects or post their own and invite others to join them.

- **CIESE** (Center for Innovation in Engineering and Science Education, www.k12science.org/materials/k12/technology/real-time-data): This organization coordinates collaborative projects that engage students in real-time data collection for a variety of scientific investigations focusing on earthquakes, air pollution, and more.
- **Out of Eden Walk** (http://learn.outofedenwalk.com): In 2013, *National Geographic* journalist Paul Salopek set out on a walk around the world, tracing the history of human migration and gathering stories along the 21,000-mile, 10-year journey. He calls his approach "slow journalism." Educators are leveraging his multimedia observations for a variety of projects about human migration, storytelling, cross-cultural understanding, global conflicts, and more. Harvard's Project Zero has created an online learning community called Out of Eden Learn where educators can connect their students in "walking parties" and exchange perspectives about their own learning journeys.

Focus on the Essential Elements of High-Quality PBL Planning

Once you have the kernel of an idea for a project, it's time to make the design decisions that will give your project structure. The Essential Project Design Elements (see pages 47–48) guide those decisions. Anticipating the learning ahead will help you map out important details. At the same time, you want to remain flexible enough to allow for modifications once the project is underway. Think of your plan as a draft blueprint rather than step-by-step instructions.

Projects vary widely when it comes to subject area and grade level. Some projects are interdisciplinary; others focus on a single subject. They might last a few weeks or continue for several months. Teachers of diverse backgrounds are able to use the same PBL framework for project planning and collaboration, regardless of content area or complexity.

★ **Gold Standard Project Based Teaching Practices: Design and Plan**

Whether you are starting with a project idea of your own, adapting an existing plan, or codesigning with students, you need to focus on key design decisions to set the stage for high-quality results. Indicators for Design and Plan from the Gold Standard Project Based Teaching Rubric include the following points:

- Project includes all Essential Project Design Elements as described on the project design rubric.

- Plans are detailed and include scaffolding and assessment of student learning and a project calendar, which remains flexible to meet student needs.

- Resources for the project have been anticipated to the fullest extent possible and arranged well in advance.

See the Appendix for the complete Project Based Teaching Rubric.

At the heart of PBL planning are the student learning goals. What should students know or be able to do by the end of the project? Answering that question will help you identify the key knowledge and understanding that you want students to acquire.

PBL experiences challenge students to think deeply and wrestle with uncertainty, so you should aim for academic goals that are sufficiently rigorous. If you could teach the content in a quick lesson or if students could Google their way to an answer, then it's not worth the time and investment required for a meaningful project.

Along with content mastery goals, consider the success skills that students also will develop or deepen through their PBL experience. Students who are able to think critically, solve problems, collaborate, and manage their own learning are well equipped for future challenges in college, careers, and citizenship. PBL provides opportunities to hone these success skills, which students will continue to use long after a project ends.

Inviting feedback from colleagues early in the planning process will improve your final project. Tuning protocols, gallery walks, and coplanning with your department or grade-level team are all tried-and-true strategies for soliciting critical feedback. Informal sharing is also valuable for helping you refine project details or set the stage for collaboration with another teacher.

To help students reach the meaningful learning goals you have identified, focus on these Essential Project Design Elements as you plan your project:

Challenging problem or question: Neither too difficult nor too easy, the right challenge or problem puts students at the edge of their comfort zone and causes them to stretch their thinking muscles. Open-ended questions and ill-structured problems allow for many possible "correct" responses or solutions.

Sustained inquiry: From project launch to final reflection, students engage in deep inquiry to make their own meaning. That means they need to be asking questions, conducting research, carrying out investigations, and weighing evidence to arrive at answers. A driving question brings the entire inquiry experience into focus and leads to learning goals. Additional student-generated questions called need-to-knows (i.e., "What do we *need to know* to answer the driving question?") help sustain inquiry throughout the project.

Authenticity: By making the learning as applicable to the real world as possible, you will up the ante when it comes to student engagement. Look for real-world connections, including

- Context. The issue or challenge isn't fake or simulated; students readily make connections to the world beyond the classroom.
- Tasks students undertake, tools they use, and the standards they refer to. These reflect how people solve problems and generate solutions in the real world.
- Impact of their work. Students see that their efforts matter.
- Connections to students' personal interests, concerns, values, and culture.

Student voice and choice: Students make decisions, and they express and defend opinions throughout the project.

Reflection: Students are prompted to think about their own learning throughout projects. Reflection prompts encourage students to consider any obstacles they are facing, challenges they have overcome, and the quality of work they are producing.

Critique and revision: Students improve their work (and deepen their learning) by engaging in cycles of critique and revision en route to final products. Formative assessment from multiple sources (including teachers, peers, and outside experts) gives students useful, actionable information to help them refine their products.

Public product: At the culmination of a project, students share their final product, solution, or argument with an audience that extends beyond the classroom. A public audience is another aspect of authenticity; students are more motivated to produce high-quality work when they know their efforts will have a real-world impact. Sharing their work with an audience can take many forms, including publishing (online or in hard copy), public forums, pitch sessions, and demonstrations. These are all authentic ways that ideas are shared in the world beyond the classroom.

To see how these Essential Project Design Elements shape the planning process, let's pick up Kimberly Head-Trotter's story and the resulting March on Nashville project.

Head-Trotter knew she wanted to leverage students' interest in the civil rights movement to help them meet academic goals and build success skills. For this project, she focused on an ELA standard that calls on students to examine historical events through texts. By having students work in teams, she also planned to develop their collaboration skills—which was the success skill she would focus on.

With those learning goals in mind, Head-Trotter's next challenge was finding the right text to anchor the learning for her diverse learners. To generate ideas, she brainstormed with her school librarian. A number of titles came up in their conversation, but one stood out.

In a graphic novel–style memoir called *March*, Congressman John Lewis shares his personal account of the civil rights movement. As Head-Trotter thought about this selection, she reflected, "A lot of my students are into graphic novels. I know they will like this. For my struggling readers, the drawings are going to help them. My high readers are going to be able to tackle this text and look closely for historical information. This choice will allow me to differentiate."

Figure 2.1   Essential Project Design Elements for Gold Standard PBL

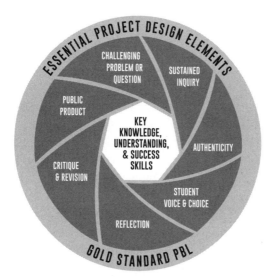

From there, Head-Trotter considered what students might produce for a culminating product that would demonstrate evidence of learning. She asked herself a series of questions, such as "What could students create while also giving them a degree of voice and choice? How could they use collaboration skills, along with reflection and revision, to support one another throughout the project?"

Once again, brainstorming with a colleague led her to a good idea. Head-Trotter's school media specialist told her about a tool called ThingLink for annotating digital content. The tool would enable students to apply what they learned about history from studying *March* and create a virtual tour of the civil rights movement in their own community. By selecting images, writing text, and combining that information with geographic locations, they could tell the story of

Nashville's own march for justice, including lunch counter sit-ins and school desegregation. Their work would be accessible to anyone with a smartphone, connecting students with an authentic audience.

Creating the annotated tour of Nashville's historic sites would also serve as a summative assessment of student learning. As artifacts of learning, students' digital products would show whether they had met the ELA standard about examining historical events through texts. Head-Trotter crafted a driving question to focus on the learning goals and give students a call to action as local historians: *How can we, as historians, design a virtual civil rights museum app that will preserve the Nashville influence on the civil rights movement?*

Head-Trotter was off and running with project design. Once she was clear about the key learning goals, driving question, and final product that would provide evidence of learning, she had what she describes as "the skeleton" of the project.

Her next design challenge was to flesh out that skeleton by considering more questions. Which other standards could she also address in the project? Which learning activities would naturally fit into the project calendar? How could she plan for formative assessment to make sure she would meet the needs of her diverse learners? How could she launch the project with high engagement, starting on day one, and sustain inquiry throughout the project? There was still plenty of planning ahead, but she was certain that March on Nashville would take her students in a meaningful direction.

❍ Try This: Consult with Experts During Project Planning

Interesting projects often put students into specific, real-world roles. For example, a driving question might ask the following questions: *How can we, as environmental scientists, create a habitat for wildlife on our playground? How can we, as artists, bring attention to social issues affecting our community? How can we apply chemistry to improve the quality of local drinking water?*

But what if you have little experience in these roles yourself? Experts whose work is related to your topic or content area can offer useful feedback during project planning. By inviting expert advice, you ensure that the project you are planning will challenge students to solve problems in the same way the pros do.

To get a better understanding of how experts work, ask them specific questions to inform your project plan. For example:

- How do you decide which questions or problems to tackle?
- How do you conduct research or gather evidence?
- Which tools are useful in your work?
- What's the role of collaboration in your field?
- What are the standards of quality in your discipline? How do you define excellence?
- How do experts in your field share or publish their results?

Where will you find experts to interview? To connect with content experts from diverse fields, start with your parent community. Ask about professions as well as hobbies. Expand your expert network by reaching out to local businesses, nearby colleges and universities, and nonprofit organizations. Don't overlook college clubs and professional organizations as sources of expertise.

The more you can bring expert ways of thinking and working into PBL, the more authentic your projects will become.

Detailed but Flexible

How much day-to-day planning should go into your PBL design? You don't want to produce a scripted lesson plan that leaves little room for student voice or choice. On the other hand, you do want to carefully consider the scaffolding, assessment plan, and calendar for your project before you launch it with students. Having those pieces in place will prepare you to manage the sometimes-messy learning that happens in a student-driven classroom.

When designing March on Nashville, for example, Kimberly Head-Trotter considered the learning activities that all of her students would take part in, starting with an entry event to launch the project. For that, she planned a field trip to the Nashville Public Library to tour a civil rights exhibit and explore primary source material with the help of a historian. "It's a way to get the students as excited about the project as I am," she says, "by putting history in the palm of their hands."

Head-Trotter also knew she would be working with students who had mixed abilities as readers. Her plan included scaffolding to help all students succeed. Early in the project, she planned to read portions of the text aloud to all students to model good reading. Later in the project, she planned to pair readers of differing abilities for specific literacy activities. "If I have a struggling reader, I might have another student read to him for a pair activity." She also planned to have audio recordings available for students who needed another way to access the content.

Similarly, when Telannia Norfar designed a high school geometry project about designing a house for a client with special requirements for her extended family, she considered the learning needs of her diverse learners. To help English language learners discuss mathematics, she prepared a list of sentence stems to help them frame their ideas. She drew up a checklist of design specifications to help her special education students focus on the requirements of the project.

"I thought I had planned all the scaffolding they would need," Norfar says, "but it still wasn't enough." Students began the project full of excitement about the design challenge, "but once they hit the math, they folded like dominoes!" From her formative assessment, Norfar could see that many students were struggling with basic math concepts. "These were concepts that they knew but had not used in a while. They needed a refresher."

She quickly shifted gears, offering students a choice for reviewing math concepts. They could get help from the teacher or from either of the two students Norfar had identified as peer helpers because they had a good grasp of the math concepts. Norfar had to revise the project calendar (Figure 2.2) to allow time for review, but it was time well spent when it came to student learning. (Read more about scaffolding student learning in Chapter 6.) For a different project with her pre-calculus students, Norfar had to modify her plan slightly when she noticed that some students were struggling to work independently. She added a weekly planning tool that asked each student to describe his or her role on the team and the tasks that needed to be done that week. At the same time, her project plan maintained flexibility for students who showed more self-direction.

"If students learned what they needed to learn and met big deadlines early, beautiful! They could use the extra time to focus on what they needed to do in other areas. I don't make up busywork for them," she says. "These are students who are close to being graduates. It's a life skill to know how you use your time well."

❷ Try This: Design a Project Calendar

A project calendar typically resembles any other calendar for planning lessons or units—but it includes several features that reflect the nature of PBL:

- An entry event on the first day(s).

- Time for team building and organizing tasks early in the project.

- Independent work time interspersed with lessons and activities.

- Plenty of time for critique and revision of work.

- Adequate time for students to practice presentation skills before making their work public.

- Time at the end of a project for reflection and celebration.

Figure 2.2 Sample Project Calendar

Project Calendar

Project: Finance Project

Time Frame: 18 Days

Monday	Tuesday	Wednesday	Thursday	Friday
		Project Week 1		
Goal(s) I can analyze parts of a complex task and identify entry points to search for a solution.	**Goal(s)** I can state different investment vehicles, interest, and a basic look of a financial plan.	**Goal(s)** I can state different investment vehicles, interest, and a basic look of a financial plan.	**Goal(s)** I can ask useful questions.	**Goal(s)** I can create an equation in one variable that represents a financial model and use it to solve a situation. I can look for and make use of structure in financial equations.
Activities/Lessons Entry Event: Introduction of client. Project teams formed and do team-builder. Students complete a problem-solving form using the gradual release model to support struggling readers and ELLs. Students review models of financial plans. Students create questions for families and investment planner.	**Activities/Lessons** Introduce students to financial planner. Financial planner explains the basics of financial planning while students take notes. Short Q&A after the presentation. Graphic organizer is provided to take notes. Project teams make agreements for completing project tasks.	**Activities/Lessons** Teams review financial plans from financial planner and use point-of-view check protocol to select a format to use for their family's financial plan. Teams complete a Charrette protocol using their chosen financial plan design. Teams adjust their plan based upon the feedback. Students examine the chosen plan and update their questions for the families.	**Activities/Lessons** Introduce students to families. Assigned students (chosen based upon their communication ability) interview the families while others take notes. Students update the problem-solving form.	**Activities/Lessons** Students work on an investigation with the support of the TI-Nspire calculator about the basic compound interest formula.
Assessments/Deliverables Student-generated questions, problem-solving form, and discussion of challenges and success with problem-solving process	**Assessments/Deliverables** Exit ticket. Updated questions for families	**Assessments/Deliverables** Updated questions for families. Financial plan format form	**Assessments/Deliverables** Discussion of interviewing process, interview intake form, journal entry and updated problem-solving form	**Assessments/Deliverables** Investigation Reflection in teams and class discussion of collaboration skills

Project Week 2

Monday	Tuesday	Wednesday	Thursday	Friday
Goal(s) I can create an equation in one variable that represents a financial model and use it to solve a situation. I can look for and make use of structure in financial equations. I can graph functions and interpret key features.	**Goal(s)** I can create an equation in one variable that represents a financial model and use it to solve a situation. I can look for and make use of structure in financial equations. I can graph functions and interpret key features.	**Goal(s)** I can create an equation in one variable that represents a financial model and use it to solve a situation. I can look for and make use of structure in financial equations. I can graph functions and interpret key features.	**Goal(s)** I can create an equation in one variable that represents a financial model and use it to solve a situation. I can look for and make use of structure in financial equations. I can graph functions and interpret key features.	**Goal(s)** I can write an explanatory plan to help a family understand how to meet their financial goals.
Activities/Lessons Students complete investigation started the previous day. Class discusses how the calculations connect to the financial plans they are to create. Teacher models calculating other financial formulas. Students practice problems using the formulas similar to their families.	**Activities/Lessons** Teacher reviews seminar norms. Students complete a Socratic seminar on financial calculations. Sentence starters and graphic organizers are used to support the discussion.	**Activities/Lessons** Teacher models an example of a financial mathematical report. Students work on their first draft of a financial report. Students give a praise, question, and suggestion about another teammate's draft.	**Activities/Lessons** Students complete their financial report using the feedback from the previous day. Project teams meet to review progress toward completing project tasks.	**Activities/Lessons** Teacher explains how to work as a team to write the plan using their financial report. Students work on their financial plan.
Assessments/Deliverables Financial calculations worksheet	**Assessments/Deliverables** Journal entry and responses in seminar	**Assessments/Deliverables** Praise-question-suggestion form	**Assessments/Deliverables** Financial report	**Assessments/Deliverables** Exit question Reflection in teams and class discussion of collaboration skills

continued

Figure 2.2   Sample Project Calendar (*continued*)

		Project Week 3		
Monday	Tuesday	Wednesday	Thursday	Friday
Flex day	**Goal(s)** I can write an explanatory plan to help a family understand how to meet their financial goals. **Activities/Lessons** Students work on their financial plan. Financial planner meets with each team to offer feedback on their progress. **Assessments/Deliverables** Exit question	**Goal(s)** I can listen to/read the plans of others, ask clarifying questions and offer suggestions to improve. **Activities/Lessons** Teacher models an adapted version of a tuning protocol using a fishbowl. Students complete the tuning protocol. **Assessments/Deliverables** Exit question and journal entry	**Goal(s)** I can write an explanatory plan to help a family understand how to meet their financial goals. **Activities/Lessons** Teams revise their proposals based upon the feedback from the tuning protocol. Teams review progress toward completing project tasks. **Assessments/Deliverables** Financial plan Reflection in teams and class discussion of collaboration skills	**Goal(s)** I can write an explanatory plan to help a family understand how to meet their financial goals. I can explain my financial plan using mathematical support to my family. **Activities/Lessons** Teams revise their proposals based upon the feedback from the tuning protocol. Teams begin to practice their presentation of the plan to the family. **Assessments/Deliverables** Financial plan

Project Week 4

Monday	Tuesday	Wednesday	Thursday	Friday
Flex day	**Goal(s)** I can explain my financial plan using mathematical support to my family. **Activities/Lessons** Teams practice presenting their plan to the family. Teams present to other teams, financial planner, or Mrs. Norfar and revise their presentation based upon the feedback. **Assessments/Deliverables** Observation of presentations	**Goal(s)** I can explain my financial plan using mathematical support to my family. **Activities/Lessons** Teams present to the families, followed by celebration and final reflections on collaboration skills and the project as a whole. **Assessments/Deliverables** Presentations Self- and peer-assessment of collaboration skills		

Source: Used with permission from Telannia Norfar, Northwest Classen High School, Oklahoma City, OK.

Resources Ready

Which resources will students need during the project? Are these resources readily available, or will they require some legwork to locate? The project planning stage is the time to anticipate resources that will be essential for project success. That includes traditional tools such as reading materials along with technologies and outside experts.

For the March on Nashville project, Kimberly Head-Trotter knew that a specific technology tool—ThingLink (www.thinglink.com)—would be essential for producing a digital map of Nashville that could be accessed from mobile devices. The tool would enable students to be content creators, annotating locations that were important during the civil rights movement, and then share their product with a public audience. However, Head-Trotter was not an expert in using the tool.

Part of her planning was recruiting the school media specialist to support students with technology use. That meant Head-Trotter didn't have to be the go-to digital expert. Students could work on their maps in the library with the media specialist available for support as they needed it.

As you consider the resources needed for your project, think about both the "stuff" students will need and the people who can provide support, advice, or information. For example:

- Technology tools may come into play throughout a project. Consider the learning goals you want to accomplish—such as research using primary sources, science simulations, or collaborative writing—and then look for digital tools that fill the purpose. To plan for meaningful integration of technology, seek support from the school media specialist, librarian, or instructional technology coach.
- Content experts often play a key role during PBL. Students may need to connect with experts during research or for technical feedback on their prototypes or proposed solutions as they refine and revise their work. To find willing experts, reach out to your parent community, businesses, nonprofits, or colleges. Be clear about what you're asking of experts, and keep their time investment limited.

- Authentic problems often connect to multiple content areas. Think about opportunities for interdisciplinary learning during project design. Reach out to teachers in other disciplines during project planning. You may be able to team up, even if only for part of a project. For example, if a social studies project calls for survey design and data analysis, this part of the project could be a chance for students to also apply what they are learning in math or statistics. Similarly, look for English language arts connections in a science project that involves writing a research brief.
- Depending on the project, students may want to take advantage of makerspaces, science labs, art studios, or music/video production studios to develop their products or prototypes. If your school does not have these facilities on site, you may be able to connect students with community resources that do, such as public libraries.

❷ Try This: Decide How to Involve Other Adults in a Project

For a relatively simple project, or for your first project if you're new to PBL, you might decide not to include any other adults besides yourself. However, to increase the project's rigor and authenticity, boost student motivation, and make real-world connections to learning, involving adults from outside the classroom really helps. They could be other teachers or school staff, parents, or—for an even greater impact—other members of the community, experts, professionals, and representatives of organizations.

There are many ways to involve adults:

- **Content experts:** Bring in guest speakers—or connect with them online—to provide information or teach students a particular skill that's needed for the project.

❷ Try This: Decide How to Involve Other Adults in a Project (*continued*)

- **Mentors:** Mentors are similar to guest speakers or experts, but they work more closely with students over a longer period of time. Several mentors could be included, working with different individuals or teams of students.

- **Audience or panel members:** Invite other adults to hear and see students make their work public, either at the culmination of a project or as formative assessment when students are creating products and developing answers to a driving question. When acting as audience members, adult experts can ask questions to probe students' understanding and work processes and play a role in assessing students' work.

- **Clients or product users:** Outside adults—or the organizations they represent—can provide the focus for a whole project (starting with the entry event) by asking students to do something or solve a problem. For example, in teacher Cheryl Bautista's tiny house project, she recruited community members to tell students what their needs were and later hear students' proposals for tiny houses for them.

When you invite adults to participate in a project, keep these tips in mind:

- Involve students, if appropriate and feasible, in finding outside adults and asking for their help.

- Make sure your "ask" is specific about their task and clear about how much time is expected.

- Ask your colleagues, personal friends, and members of the parent community for connections they might have to other adult professionals, experts, and organizations. Don't be afraid to reach out, even without a connection, since most people are glad to help if they can!

Beyond the Basics: Designing for Equity and Impact

Additional design decisions help foster important goals of equity and impact in PBL. Telannia Norfar considers all of the Essential Project Design Elements when planning projects, but she doesn't stop there. Three more considerations factor into her planning process, especially when she's planning projects for students who are below grade level, have limited background experiences, or are English language learners. As she explains,

> First, I always want to expose my students to some aspect of math that's applicable to a career they could have. In precalculus, they learn about the work of financial planners and start to see themselves in that role. In geometry, an obvious career connection is the field of design. By designing a house, students will have to apply geometry concepts and also see that they have the potential to be an architect.

> Second, I don't want students' limited background knowledge to be a barrier. That means the project has to be accessible to everyone. Whether kids live in apartments or in houses, they've all experienced residences. They have some schema. We don't have to build a lot of background about what a "home" means.

> Third, when working with students of mixed ability levels, I want everyone to be able to engage. They all need to be able to have a place where they can grasp and grow.

Similarly, teacher Ray Ahmed wants his students—most of whom are living in poverty and many of whom have special needs—to learn to advocate for themselves. "We've noticed as a community that our kids don't know how to advocate for themselves. That has kept them from being successful in high school, in college, and outside school. We need to teach them [to advocate] in the context of a classroom." Ahmed uses conferencing as one PBL scaffolding strategy to encourage students to speak up for themselves.

"When kids come to conference, they know it will be based on an issue, problem, or challenge that they have identified. They have thought about a couple solutions, but they need help thinking it through." With repeat practice, student confidence increases. "We see kids going off to college more confident about talking with their professors if they're struggling. They've practiced doing this as kids and come to value having that agency." (Read more about Ahmed's use of conferences in Chapter 6.)

For middle school teacher Rebecca Newburn, one more consideration comes into play. She wants students to come away from science projects feeling empowered to make wise decisions in the future. She wants them to know how to have an effect on issues that matter to them.

"I could explain in a lecture why climate change is an important issue," she says, "but students are likely to tune out. I want them to connect to the issue and to ask deeper questions. What does this [content] have to do with the way I live my life? What choice can I make that will make a difference?"

By the end of a project, Newburn looks for evidence of enduring understanding in science. She also wants students to be able to identify what action they can take. "They may not remember every detail about thermal energy," she acknowledges, "but they understand the big picture well enough to ask good questions and think critically."

Coaches' Notebook: How to Lend an Ear During PBL Planning

Providing teachers with practical feedback during the Design and Plan phase is a useful role for instructional coaches. James Fester, PBL teacher turned coach, worked with middle school teacher Rebecca Newburn to help her think through her plans for an ambitious project about climate change.

He shared some observations about how their collaboration—and his questioning—led to a better-designed project:

As I coach, I am often a nonexpert in the subject matter. I used to be a history teacher. What do I know about math or science? And Rebecca is clearly an expert in her content. Together, we can hash out the details. We know that if her plan makes sense to me, it will make sense to her students.

Each time we sat down to work together, I would ask, "What do you want students to know by the end of the day (or the end of the project)?" Then, together, we could look for practical ways to help students get to understanding and arrive at conclusions *on their own*. How is she going to keep them engaged in learning through inquiry, figuring things out? I keep asking that question because that's the sweet spot for PBL.

One of her goals was for students to have more discourse about science. We thought about discussion protocols that have students using academic language. She had the idea of putting little tents on the tables that have sentence stems. That's brilliant! If you want kids to have good discussions, give them what they need to stay focused.

Another idea we talked about is making sure the project meets the unique needs of middle schoolers. You really have to think about your cast of characters. What are their developmental needs? We know that middle schoolers put a premium on socialization. So, any protocols that get them talking, chatting about content, being interactive—those activities are not just important but actually essential for learning at this age. Without those prompts, they'll find other things to talk about.

We looked at her project calendar and talked about when the last time was that students had a chance to get up and chat with someone. When have you planned for them to orally share what's going on with their learning? We kept revising the plan to incorporate those activities regularly.

Collaborative planning of this type doesn't require extensive blocks of time. Fester and Newburn were able to make significant progress by finding 15-minute opportunities for mini-consultations and using the time efficiently. "At the end of each session, we would talk about our action steps. What did each of us need to do before we met again?" Fester recalls. "That proved to be a key norm for our partnership."

Reuse and Refresh Your Own Projects

Teachers who are new to PBL often wonder if they will have to start from scratch with project planning every school year. The short answer is no. Many projects are evergreen and suitable to use again and again. Others may need to be refreshed so the content remains timely and relevant. PBL veterans make it a practice to reflect on their projects and invite feedback from colleagues and students about how to make them better next time.

Two veteran PBL teachers in Davis, California, decided that "good" wasn't good enough. After taking a critical look at a popular interdisciplinary project called America at War, they remodeled it to deepen academic understanding and expand connections to the community. "This transitioned from a decent but kind of small, narrowly focused project to something big and broad," reflects Tyler Millsap, who teaches both English and history at DaVinci Charter Academy.

Initially, the project challenged students to analyze war novels and apply their understanding of U.S. history to create film pilots for the "next great war movie." English teacher Scott Stephen Bell saw opportunities to introduce new novels coming out of recent conflicts in Iraq and Afghanistan. Contemporary reading choices—such as *Generation Kill, Jarhead,* and *The Watch*—indeed proved appealing to students and allowed for differentiation based on reading levels.

Despite high student engagement, teachers worried that the history side of the project was too thin. "We would talk generally about foreign policy and the causes of conflicts," Millsap says, "but there wasn't a driving purpose to it."

The opportunity for project remodeling came along when Millsap happened to call a local congressman's office on an unrelated matter: "His aide told me about the Veterans History Project at the Library of Congress. The congressman was interested in having high school students interview local veterans to get their stories. Would we be interested?" After pausing a heartbeat to consider how much extra legwork this might entail, Millsap agreed—and has never looked back.

"This has become one of the biggest pieces of the project," he says. "Students get partnered with U.S. military veterans, conduct an interview, and create a primary source document that goes to the Library of Congress. Knowing that they have an authentic audience is huge for students."

If you are remodeling a project from previous years, ask yourself the following questions:

- What went well with the most recent implementation of this project? Even if you plan to make changes or modifications, be sure to identify the successful aspects that you want to retain.
- Where were the weak spots in the past? How can you troubleshoot specific challenges with additional scaffolding, more formative assessment, or different learning activities?
- Does the content need to be refreshed to be more timely or relevant to students' lives?
- Are there opportunities to make community connections that will increase student engagement?
- Do you see opportunities to make the project more cross-disciplinary? Do you have a colleague from another content area who wants to team up?

Strategies to Design and Plan High-Quality Projects: Key Takeaways

In this chapter, you have encountered several strategies and resources to help you design and plan effective projects. Take time to think about the following points:

- How do the Essential Project Design Elements for Gold Standard PBL change or influence your thinking about instructional design? Which elements are already evident in your classroom? Which will require more attention from you?
- Which of the strategies for finding project ideas (described on pages 39–44) resonate with you?
- How comfortable are you with involving students in project planning?
- Where will you find opportunities to invite feedback from colleagues about projects you are planning? How might you leverage strategies such as gallery walks or peer critique protocols to invite feedback on your plans?

On Your PBL Bookshelf

PBL Starter Kit: To-the-Point Advice, Tools and Tips for Your First Project in Middle or High School (2nd ed.), and *PBL in the Elementary Grades: Step-by-Step Guidance, Tools and Tips for Standards-Focused K–5 Projects*: These two publications from the Buck Institute for Education provide readers with practical advice and tools to plan and facilitate PBL, with an emphasis on the essential elements for project design. John Larmer is the principal author of the *PBL Starter Kit*; Sara wHallerman and John Larmer are the principal authors for the elementary version.

Real-World Projects: How Do I Design Relevant and Engaging Learning Experiences? In this short-format book, Suzie Boss outlines strategies for increasing the authenticity of projects to increase student engagement in learning.

Students at the Center: Personalized Learning with Habits of Mind: Bena Kallick and Allison Zmuda bring clarity to discussions of personalized learning by focusing on four attributes: student voice, cocreation, social construction, and self-discovery. Examples illustrate how to design learning experiences that students will find personally meaningful.

3

Align to Standards

*Align projects to meaningful academic goals to ensure
that PBL is "main course" learning and not dessert.*

For more than a decade, Erin Brandvold has been teaching in schools
that embrace Project Based Learning. "I feel lucky," she says. "Even
my student teaching was in PBL settings." She currently teaches world
history at Impact Academy of Arts and Technology in Hayward, California. The school serves a diverse population, including many students growing up in poverty. Most graduates will be the first in their
families to attend college.

Brandvold can see how one Project Based Teaching Practice
in particular has helped improve outcomes for her students—all of
whom are college bound. "Several years ago, we used to just do cool
projects. Students enjoyed them, but sometimes we wondered, what
were we really teaching? What were the ideas and skills my students
needed to know and be able to do? Over time," she says, "we've got-
ten better at designing projects to showcase those things that are
worth knowing."

A good example is a 10th grade world history project called
Revolutions on Trial. In planning the six-week project, Brandvold
carefully considered learning goals related to both historical content
about revolutions and Common Core State Standards about claims
and counterclaims. Throughout the project, from project launch until
the mock trial that served as a culminating event, she deliberately

aligned learning activities and assessments to those target standards. That gave students a clear understanding of what they needed to learn and why those ideas are worth knowing.

> ◼ A companion video about aligning projects to standards can be found at www.bie.org.

Why Align Projects to Standards?

When teachers align PBL to standards, they ensure that the learning experience is going to be worth the investment of time. Academic rigor is built in from the outset, especially if teachers align projects to priority standards. That means, rather than aiming for lower-level learning targets that could be addressed in a lesson or two, projects should align to standards that get at big ideas, involve complexity, and call for higher-order thinking.

Focusing on high-priority standards enables you to build deep, conceptual understanding rather than racing to cover a list of discrete facts that students may quickly forget. Priority standards (sometimes called "power standards") typically incorporate related learning goals. Knowing how to write an effective essay, for example, requires mastery of vocabulary, spelling, and grammar (Ainsworth, 2014a). A project that emphasizes essay writing will also teach those related skills. Similarly, a math project that builds understanding of the properties of quadrilaterals might not address every four-sided shape under the sun. Go ahead and "punt the rhombus," advises assessment expert Douglas Reeves, and keep your focus on the priority standards (Ainsworth, 2014a, p. 10).

Although Erin Brandvold's school gives her considerable latitude when it comes to curriculum planning, many PBL teachers must follow a district-mandated scope and sequence. Some districts also give regularly scheduled benchmark tests, which focus on specific learning targets, as often as every nine weeks. Integrating PBL with district mandates can be done, but it requires careful planning.

Lanier High School in Gwinnett County, Georgia, is a good example. Students who are part of the school's Center for Design and Technology (CDAT) not only tackle ambitious projects, often with business partners, but also must take state and districtwide tests. With careful alignment to standards by CDAT teachers, students consistently score at high levels on standardized tests and also boast such real-world PBL accomplishments as earning patents for their inventions or film credits for their role in creating video animations for professional productions.

Aligning to standards naturally overlaps with other Project Based Teaching Practices, especially Design and Plan (Chapter 2). The deliberate focus on standards doesn't just happen at the design stage, however. The driving question, project rubric, entry event, scaffolding, public products, and assessment plan all align to targeted standards.

★ Gold Standard Project Based Teaching Practices: Align to Standards

When projects are thoughtfully aligned to standards, you will see evidence that teachers are clearly communicating learning goals and helping students reach them. Indicators from the Gold Standard Project Based Teaching Rubric for Align to Standards include the following points:

- Criteria for products are clearly and specifically derived from standards and allow demonstration of mastery.

- Scaffolding of student learning, critique and revision protocols, assessments, and rubrics consistently refer to and support student achievement of specific standards.

See the Appendix for the complete Project Based Teaching Rubric.

Aligning to What's Worth Knowing:
A Good Fit for the Revolutions Project

Let's take a closer look at how Erin Brandvold aligns projects to standards to achieve meaningful learning for her students.

Before launching into any project planning, Brandvold first unpacks all the content standards and skills her students need to master. "I ask myself, 'How will I teach those skills and concepts over the course of the year?' Then I backward-map the entire school year from the standards, identifying content and skills that I need to teach."

That yearlong content map helps Brandvold focus on where she needs to go with her students. As mentioned, some districts do this curriculum mapping for teachers by mandating a scope and sequence. Whether you are mapping out the curriculum yourself or following your district's lead, your goal is the same: look for meaningful PBL opportunities throughout the academic year by aligning projects to standards.

Brandvold's 10th grade world history students focus on the big idea of global power and resistance. That means examining "how we experience power in our daily lives and how we participate in and respond to that power," Brandvold explains. Course content helps students explore different forms of power throughout the world and how people have resisted power throughout history. Through their exploration of content, students "develop independent research skills, critical thinking, and verbal and written communication, and they become confident readers who can analyze and assess a variety of texts."

With that big picture in mind, Brandvold is ready to align projects to more specific learning goals. Based on her curriculum map, for example, she knows she will focus on argumentative writing during the second semester. That makes the revolutions project a good fit.

"I had done this project in the past using a debate as the final product. By changing it up to end in a mock trial, I thought students would have to use argumentative skills to look more closely at different perspectives," she explains. To add authenticity, she brings in legal experts to talk about how they prepare for trials. "Using that expert lens, students should be able to build stronger arguments backed up by evidence."

The project challenges students to present the case of *Citizens v. Revolutions* as a performance of their understanding. To prepare for the mock trial, they have to consider why revolutions happen and then make a compelling case about who benefits from political uprisings. For the culminating event, some students are lawyers, and others testify as witnesses. Nevertheless, all need to demonstrate effective argumentation.

To clarify the learning goals embedded in the project, Brandvold rewrote standards as "I can" statements to emphasize personal mastery. For example, some of the goals aligned to Common Core State Standards are as follows:

- I can introduce precise claim(s).
- I can distinguish the claims from alternative or opposing claims.
- I can develop claims and counterclaims fairly.
- I can point out the strengths and limitations of my claims/ counterclaims.
- I can use words, phrases, and clauses to clarify the relationships between claim(s) and counterclaims.
- I can anticipate the audience's knowledge level and concerns.
- I can provide a conclusion that follows and supports the information presented.

Other goals aligned to world history content include the following:

- I can use the revolution framework to determine the causes of revolutions.
- I can compare the Russian Revolution to another revolution.
- I can analyze the effects of dictatorships on their people.
- I can analyze the motives behind revolutionaries' actions.
- I can determine the effectiveness of revolutions in improving the lives of citizens.

Before introducing these learning goals to her classes, Brandvold wanted to make sure students were fully engaged in the topic. To build student interest, she launched the revolutions project with a weeklong simulation called Nation X.

"Students came in on day one and found the classroom set up differently," she explains. "There was a jail, a store, and areas reserved for workers. Students were placed in groups of three or four that were unequal. The royalty had a couch, had special privileges, and were paid big stacks of (fake) money," whereas the workers had only meager provisions. With the stage set for conflict, students were challenged to create a fair and functional society.

Among her four classes of world history students, different dramas unfolded that week. One class plotted an assassination attempt. In another, the leader abdicated authority altogether. One class seemed to be making progress when students called for a town meeting to agree on rules, but then, according to Brandvold, "they all started talking over each other and got frustrated."

From the teacher's vantage point, the immersive entry event experience served its purpose. Students were clearly engaged in the activity and had fresh insights into the social, political, and economic unrest that can lead to revolutions. By the end of the simulation, they were able to reflect on the experience and come to a concise definition of *revolution*. They also had a host of questions about how societies rebuild after uprisings.

Brandvold waited until the second week of the project—after the simulation concluded—to introduce students to the driving question: *How can we, as historians, determine the effectiveness of a revolution in improving the lives of citizens?*

The project unfolded with both individual and team assignments. Brandvold made sure that students understood the learning goals. To break down big goals into manageable chunks, she posted a specific learning outcome in class each day. For example, this outcome is from the second week of the project when students were building background knowledge: *I can identify the conditions, beliefs, and triggers of a revolution.* By the end of the third week, after students had spent considerable class time learning to source documents and evaluate evidence, the outcome was *I can write an argument and support it with convincing evidence.*

At the end of each class period, students scored themselves from 1 to 4 on how well they had met that day's outcome. This formative self-assessment helped Brandvold plan follow-up lessons tailored to students' specific learning needs. (Read more about the assessments in this project in Chapter 5.)

Brandvold's use of daily targets reflects her own belief that learning should be purposeful. When students are clued in to the learning targets, she says, "you avoid the question of why are we doing this? Students can see how those daily targets are tied to their final product. When you put the learning goals in context, students are more clear about the purpose of what we're doing."

❷ Try This: Determine Which Standards to Focus On

Teachers who use PBL all or most of the time find ways to include most of the standards they need to teach within projects. Teachers who use PBL less extensively may not include certain standards within projects, instead teaching them via other instructional strategies. Deciding which standards to teach in a project depends a lot on your own school context, personal perspective, students, grade level or course, and other factors. There is no hard-and-fast rule, so try the following reflective process:

1. Make a table with these three categories:

   • Important and appropriate for addressing in a project.

   • Important but not appropriate for addressing in a project.

   • Not important and not appropriate for addressing in a project.

2. Place each standard you need to teach during a quarter, semester, or school year in one of the three categories by considering the following questions:

   • Is it an *important* standard? Does your district or state identify it as a "key" standard? Is it fundamental to learning in the subject

⊘ Try This: Determine Which Standards to Focus On (*continued*)

area? Is it a core or crosscutting concept (e.g., number sense in the lower grades; mathematical modeling, systems thinking, or interpreting informational texts in higher grades)?

- Is it *appropriate* to teach via a project? Does it call for in-depth understanding and exploration? Is it complex (e.g., separation of powers in a democracy, an ecosystem), or is it relatively simple? Does it require significant time to learn, as opposed to something that could be learned in one or two lessons? (For example, lab safety procedures in science, though important, would probably not be appropriate for PBL. Neither would learning what a rhombus is, although this concept could be included in a larger math project.)

3. Consider how much time and weight will be given to each standard included in a project.

- Will this standard be in the *foreground* of the project? Will several lessons or activities be devoted to it? Will students spend considerable time learning this standard? Will it be woven throughout the project? Will it be a focus of critique, reflection, and assessment?

- Can the standard be learned during the project but relatively quickly? Can it be included within other lessons or part of the assessment of a project product—but not a major part?

- Should the standard be in the *background* of the project? Can students still be expected to practice or demonstrate the standard but not focus on it explicitly during the project?

Keep the Focus

Teachers who are new to PBL often ask how they can encourage student inquiry but still keep the focus on learning goals. What happens if students' questions or ideas take them far afield from the target standards?

Math teacher Telannia Norfar deliberately guides students toward standards by making sure every learning activity in a project connects to desired learning goals. "I want to make sure the standards show up over and over again," she says. "And that's so easy *not* to do if you aren't careful!"

For example, in her geometry project about home design, students knew they needed to make a blueprint to present to their client. Some students wanted to start with an online tool that would have produced nice-looking results. "It will *look* like they did something wonderful, but where's the math in that? The tool does all the calculations for you in the background," Norfar says. To make sure students were hitting their learning goals, she had them do their first blueprint drafts by hand. "That's where we'll see the math," she explains. Later in the project, once students had demonstrated their math competency, they had the option of using an online tool to produce the final blueprints.

Avoiding "scope creep" is another strategy to keep projects from getting unwieldy. Rather than piling on more and more standards as the project gets underway, keep the focus on the learning goals you want to emphasize. Help students see how the driving question and final product align to those learning goals. Each time you return to the need-to-know list for a class discussion, for example, ask students to consider whether their questions are essential to answering the driving question.

At times, you may need to rein in student ideas that take them far afield of project goals. Some teachers use a "parking lot" on a whiteboard or project board to capture student questions or suggestions that are worth investigating—just not right now!

Reflection prompts can also help maintain focus on learning goals. For example, you might have students reflect on their progress toward mastery of specific skills or understanding, using the project rubric as a reference. An elementary teacher has her students color-code the rubric to show their progress over time—moving from yellow (for emerging) to orange (for developing) to green (for proficiency).

Coaches' Notebook: Connect Across Disciplines

Real-world problems tend to be complicated. Solutions often require experts from different disciplines to pool their thinking, building on or sometimes challenging one another's ideas. To make PBL more authentic, it makes sense to look for interdisciplinary content connections.

Getting started with collaborative project planning can be a challenge, acknowledges instructional coach James Fester. Especially at the secondary level, teachers are usually experts in their own subjects but may have trouble finding standards-based connections with other subject areas.

To jump-start interdisciplinary project planning, here are three of his tried-and-true coaching methods (Fester, 2017).

Mind Mapping: This method is especially effective for teachers who are already part of a collaborative team or know with whom they want to team up on a project. The process begins with each teacher creating a mind map of the major themes and standards they teach throughout the year on a large piece of poster paper (see Figure 3.1). These posters are then hung up on the wall, and each teacher takes a turn narrating his or her course of study, one standard at a time. While one teacher speaks, the others listen and look for connections to their own subject areas. Whenever they hear something similar to what they do, they mark or annotate the speaker's poster silently to take note of the connection. After each teacher has had a chance to narrate his or her poster, the team should have several annotations that reveal connection points that can then be used as the starting point for fleshing out a great project.

Driving Questions Gallery Walk: This method works especially well at staff meetings or with teachers who don't yet have a designated team or project partner. It begins with writing 15 to 20 driving questions on a large piece of poster paper. Hang these on the walls of the meeting space to create a gallery. Teachers are then asked to conduct a silent gallery walk where they read each driving question, consider possible connections to their own area of study, and write the connections on the poster as a way of sharing them with the rest of the room.

Figure 3.1   Mind Map for Making Cross-Curricular Connections

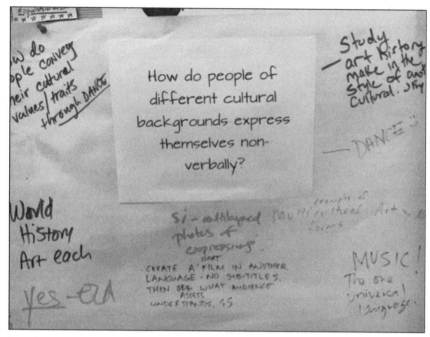

Source: Used with permission from James Fester.

If teachers don't see any overt alignment to their standards, they can offer revisions to the driving question to make it more relevant to their field of study. They then move to the next poster and repeat the process. At the end of this protocol, teachers revisit the posters with questions they felt were particularly relevant and discuss the connections and possible entry points for project planning.

Hint: Ideas for driving questions can be generated by teachers, students, or instructional coaches, or by borrowing from project libraries for inspiration.

Time Line: This planning protocol is designed for smaller teams or pairs of teachers looking for cross-curricular planning opportunities within a specific part of the school year, such as the last semester.

It starts with each teacher taking a stack of sticky notes and writing out a calendar one day (or week) at a time—with one sticky note representing one day (or week). These notes are then affixed to a wall or table in a long line, while the partner teacher does the same. Ultimately, the two calendars are parallel to each other. After the calendars have been posted, the teachers look at their partner's calendar and try to find places where their content potentially overlaps. Teachers are encouraged to look for places where they can move their sticky notes to make stronger connections to their partner's subject matter or to create opportunities to support a project their partner may be doing.

Strategies for Aligning to Standards: Key Takeaways

In this chapter, you read about a range of strategies to help you align projects to standards. Take time to reflect on your current practice, and consider opportunities to make stronger connections between standards and the learning goals of your projects:

- How much flexibility do you have when it comes to standards? Do you do curriculum mapping yourself, or are you expected to follow a district or schoolwide scope and sequence? How do school or system directives influence your PBL planning?
- When you look at the content goals for the entire school year in your subject or grade level, where do you see the best opportunities for projects that can address the big ideas of your content area?
- When you consider your curriculum map, where do you see the best opportunities for interdisciplinary projects?
- How explicit are you in explaining learning goals to students? How might more clarity about daily goals help your students manage their learning?

On Your PBL Bookshelf

Learning Targets: Helping Students Aim for Understanding in Today's Lesson: Connie M. Moss and Susan M. Brookhart explain how learning targets can be used by teachers, students, and school leaders to create a culture of achievement. They offer strategies for designing daily learning targets to encourage student goal setting and self-regulation.

Prioritizing the Common Core: Identifying Specific Standards to Emphasize the Most: Larry Ainsworth guides readers through the challenge of determining which standards to emphasize in instruction and assessment to help students master important concepts at a deep level.

Understanding by Design (2nd ed.): Grant Wiggins and Jay McTighe pioneered the concept of "backward design" or "starting with the end in mind" when it comes to instructional design. Their UbD framework, informed by years of fieldwork and teacher feedback, is consistent with best practices for PBL design.

4

Manage Activities

Well-managed PBL enables students to get to deeper learning and develop the success skills that will serve them well in the project—and in life.

Teacher Jim Bentley and his students at Foulks Ranch Elementary School in Elk Grove, California, have earned a well-deserved reputation as filmmakers. When city officials in their hometown need instructional films to educate their community about recycling, they have repeatedly "hired" Bentley's students as producers. In recognition of the effort involved, the city awards service-learning grants to the school.

During the 2016–17 school year, Bentley's 6th graders took on the request of creating seven short videos to educate the local business community about a new state law requiring the recycling of organic waste. The law is gradually being phased in; by 2020, most small business owners and apartment managers will need to have a recycling program in place to divert food scraps and other organic waste from local landfills.

Authentic projects such as this deliver multiple wins. Having a real client ensures high engagement and sets the stage for memorable learning. With a public audience guaranteed, students (and their teacher) set a high bar for themselves when it comes to quality, creativity, and productivity. Bentley is able to align film projects to rigorous standards across the curriculum, including science, literacy, math, social studies, and technology.

▉ A companion video about managing activities can be found at www.bie.org.

To make sure that student filmmakers deliver high-quality products on schedule—and to maximize learning opportunities along the way—Bentley has to be skillful at project management. "My job is to make sure this isn't just an activity," the veteran PBL teacher explains. "I need to bring in the big ideas [of content areas], work with seven different student teams producing seven different films, and stick with a pretty ambitious time line."

The projects that Bentley and his students tackle are admittedly complex and time-intensive, which reflect the teacher's depth of experience with PBL. Newcomers would be wise to start with less ambitious projects (which is exactly how Bentley built his own confidence as a Project Based Teacher). Still, even projects that require less time and perhaps address only one content area also require thoughtful attention to management to keep the learning experience on track.

Developing your tool kit of project management strategies will help you and your students keep the process and logistics of PBL running smoothly so you can devote more attention to learning goals. To better understand how Project Based Teaching Practices support successful project management, let's take a closer look at key strategies and tools.

★ **Gold Standard Project Based Teaching Practices: Manage Activities**

During a well-managed PBL experience, teachers keep learning on track in a variety of ways. Indicators to Manage Activities from the Gold Standard Project Based Teaching Rubric include the following points:

★ **Gold Standard Project Based Teaching Practices: Manage Activities (*continued*)**

- The classroom features an appropriate mixture of individual and team work time, including both whole-group and small-group instruction.

- Well-balanced teams are formed according to the nature of the project and student needs, with appropriate student voice and choice.

- Project management tools (group calendar, team contracts, learning logs, and so forth) are used to support student self-management and independence, as well as collaboration.

- Classroom routines and norms are consistently followed during project work time to maximize productivity.

- Realistic schedules, checkpoints, and deadlines are set but flexible; no bottlenecks impede workflow.

See the Appendix for the complete Project Based Teaching Rubric.

Making the Most of Teamwork

By design, most projects involve some level of collaboration. Students engage in peer learning activities and provide one another with feedback even if they are working on individual products. The emphasis on teams in PBL is intentional, as they harness the social power of learning. It's not teamwork for the sake of teamwork, however. Collaboration is part of the authenticity of PBL, reflecting how problem solving unfolds in fields as diverse as health care, engineering, publishing, and the nonprofit sector. As complexity increases, collaboration among specialists becomes increasingly important.

Today's students will be entering an economy where collaboration is the new normal. To tackle complex challenges in our interconnected world, they will need to know how to navigate cultural differences, understand diverse perspectives, and make connections across disciplines. Teams have become the fundamental unit of organization everywhere from start-ups to government agencies to schools (Duhigg, 2016).

Excelling at teamwork is a goal that extends far beyond the classroom. Tech giant Google, for example, tried to reverse engineer the perfect team with an investigation called Project Aristotle. Google team members were surprised to learn that there is no magic formula for mixing personalities or skills to boost team productivity. Rather, as the following account shows, the answers align with effective Project Based Teaching Practices—especially, building the culture:

> The researchers eventually concluded that what distinguished the "good" teams from the dysfunctional groups was how teammates treated one another. The right norms, in other words, could raise a group's collective intelligence, whereas the wrong norms could hobble a team, even if, individually, all the members were exceptionally bright. (Duhigg, 2016, para. 28)

What's more, the higher performing teams tended to share two characteristics. First, everybody got an equal amount of airtime in team discussions (something that PBL protocols also emphasize). Second, good teams showed a high degree of social sensitivity. That's a "fancy way of saying they were skilled at intuiting how others felt based on their tone of voice, their expressions, and other nonverbal cues" (Duhigg, 2016, para. 31). Attending to those cues helped build psychological safety so that team members felt free to speak up and take risks. The same holds true in PBL classrooms where all students know they have a voice and that their ideas will be treated with respect.

Students who are new to PBL sometimes ask, "Why can't I just work alone?" Be ready to explain your reasoning about why teamwork is essential to project success. Here are a few examples of project scenarios that demand collaboration:

- A project may call for specialization. It may be too big or too complicated for one person to tackle solo. That sets the stage for students to take on specialized roles within a team, contributing their strengths to the shared effort. (See the Try This box on pages 86–87, "Have Students Take on Roles in Project Teams.")
- Driving questions are deliberately open-ended and can't be answered by a quick Google search. In fact, there are likely to be multiple "right" solutions or final products. That means students can form teams that best match their interests, reinforcing student voice and choice.
- Creativity or cultural competence may be essential to project success. Students will get to better solutions by bringing diverse perspectives, empathy, and insights to a problem or challenge. That's another real-world reason for collaboration.

When you design and plan a project (as discussed in Chapter 2), you should consider how and why students will collaborate. Will you assign teams, or will students choose their own partners? There are pros and cons to both approaches, as shown in Figure 4.1.

Another consideration is *when* to form teams. With some projects, teamwork starts right after project launch. This gives you time to deliberately teach, reinforce, and assess collaboration skills throughout the project. In other situations, you may want students to do some initial research and build understanding individually before deciding on the specific topic they want to investigate in more depth. Teams would then form naturally around those topics, giving students more voice and choice. Both strategies have merit; the key teaching move is to match your team strategy to the needs of the project and to your students' readiness when it comes to working in teams.

Once the project is underway, it's time to monitor and adjust your plan for collaboration. If students are accustomed to working individually, they will likely need your help learning to collaborate, negotiate, reach consensus, and share the workload. That's why managing team dynamics is such a crucial aspect of Project Based Teaching.

Figure 4.1 Pros and Cons of Various Approaches to Forming Teams

Approach to Forming Teams	Pros	Cons
Teacher decides	• Saves time. • Reduces disagreements and hurt feelings. • Allows teacher to balance teams for student growth and maximum effectiveness. • Is authentic; most real-world teams do not get to self-select.	• Some students may be disgruntled about their team. • Students may lose sense of ownership and buy-in. • Students do not have opportunity to learn how to choose teammates wisely.
Teacher decides, with student input	• Minimizes disagreements and hurt feelings. • Still allows teacher to balance teams for student growth and maximum effectiveness. • Students have some sense of ownership and buy-in. • Students have some opportunity to learn how to choose teammates wisely.	• Takes more teacher time. • Can be difficult to honor all students' preferences. • Some students may still be disgruntled about their team.
Teacher manages process for students to decide	• Almost eliminates disagreements. • Students have sense of ownership and buy-in. • Students have opportunity to learn how to choose teammates wisely.	• Potentially takes more time if students need to be taught how to choose teams. • Classroom culture needs to be right, to prevent issues with cliques and socially marginalized students. • There's some potential for hurt feelings. • Is not advised for very young students. • Students may not realize what capabilities are needed for the team to be effective.

When his students are tackling complex chemistry projects, teacher Ray Ahmed reminds students why effective collaboration is essential for getting desired results. For a project about water quality, for example, each student on a team carried out the same lab experiments but used a different corrosive inhibitor than the other teammates were using. "When they're collecting their data, they have to be precise," Ahmed explains. "They have to be accurate. And they also have to work together as a team because each student contributes results to the rest of the team. They have four different sources of data they're pulling from and are expected to analyze. They can't just do what they want. They have to put their own needs aside and say, 'This is the long-term goal of our team, and this is how we're going to do it.' They have to collaborate."

To build collaboration skills with her primary students, Sara Lev started with a warm-up activity. Before her 5-year-olds teamed up to work on a project with their classmates, they collaborated with "buddies" from 5th grade. Their team challenge was to build something original from recycled materials. Later, Lev debriefed the experience just with her students. They looked at a collaboration rubric specially tailored for young learners with emojis instead of more typical assessment language. (The early elementary collaboration rubric is available at www.bie.org/object/document/k_2_teamwork_rubric.)

Explains Lev, "We talked about how we could get better at being part of a team. What if it's hard to share your ideas? What if a teammate wants to go to recess instead of contributing? Where could we all find room to grow?" When students self-assessed their collaboration skills, Lev admired their honesty. "They didn't all give themselves smiley faces!" Together, they had developed a shared understanding of collaboration that carried right into their PBL work.

❯ Try This: Have Students Take on Roles in Project Teams

Project teams often work better when members have assigned roles. For older students, roles could be determined by the team, with or without the teacher. For younger students, the teacher should definitely help decide roles. Here are some suggestions that can help with assigning roles:

- Have students complete a learner profile. There are many ways to do this, but one that's been used effectively is the SING process, developed by PBL teacher/coach Kelly Reseigh for Denver Public Schools, in which students fill in answers (with help from the teacher, if needed) to prompts in four quadrants of a chart:
  - What are your **S**trengths?
  - What are your **I**nterests?
  - What are your **N**eeds?
  - What are your **G**oals?

Figure 4.2 shows an elementary example, and Figure 4.3 shows a secondary-level example. Use the results of the SING process to assign students to teams or to help older students inform their decisions about what teams they want to form.

- Decide whether to have the same roles for all projects or roles that are different depending on the project. Alternatively, you could have a mix of both, since one project might require, say, a video producer but another project would not.

- To avoid the "divide and conquer" strategy that teams might take instead of truly collaborating, think of roles in which students are in charge of *delegating* work rather than doing it all themselves. Instead of traditional "group work" roles—such as team leader, note taker, researcher, writer, and artist—consider real-world roles, such as project manager, lead engineer or historian, communications manager, social media director, and creative director. This approach also helps avoid the problems that can arise when a team has one "boss" who may either take over too much of the work or otherwise not lead a team effectively.

- Specify the tasks each role is to perform—a process than can be done with students. In traditional group work, one student might be assigned to be an artist responsible for creating illustrations. By contrast, in a PBL project team, that role might be called creative director and be responsible for ensuring creative standards are met, overseeing the creative process, quality checking for visual supports, and ensuring all creative options are voiced.

Figure 4.2   Team Roles for an Early Elementary Project

Source: Used with permission from Sara Lev.

Figure 4.3   SING (Strengths, Interests, Needs, Goals) Chart
for Creating Learner Profiles

Strengths	Interests
• Creates connections between members of a group. • Ensures that all voices are heard. • Is flexible. • Is comfortable figuring out new technology tools.	• Understands others' perspectives and experiences. • Designs unique pathways/solutions. • Integrates visual arts into work.
Needs	**Goals**
• Processes ideas by talking with others. • Creates a safe space to challenge ideas. • Identifies purpose/clear outcomes.	• Learn to balance collaboration and efficiency. • Improve organization and time management. • Provide constructive feedback to team members.

Source: Used with permission from Kelly Reseigh, Denver Public Schools.

Here are some additional strategies that will help students learn how to work well together. When students learn to collaborate effectively, they are able to produce higher quality results than they might have been able to accomplish individually.

Get off to a strong start: Whether you have assigned teams yourself or given students a choice of partners, you want to make sure teams get off to a good start. A team-building activity can help, especially if students don't yet know one another well. Low-stakes tasks such as coming up with a team name or logo can help teams form a shared identity. Introduce conversation starters or conduct surveys that help students recognize the strengths that each person brings to the team.

Encourage accountability: A team contract or agreement that describes members' responsibilities will help to build accountability. In fact, writing a team agreement can be a good team-building activity. If students are new to PBL, you might give them a template for a contract or share examples that other students have written. Encourage students to use clear, simple language (not legalese!). See Figure 4.4 for an example.

Model desired behaviors: Model what it means to be an effective member of a team. For example, you might collaborate with teaching specialists, library staff, or media specialists to plan and implement projects. Highlight the expertise each person brings and let students see how your collaboration yields better results.

Highlight real-world examples of collaboration: Help students recognize the value of teamwork in examples from outside school. Look for evidence of collaboration in news stories about scientific breakthroughs, community problem solving, or even sporting events. If you are planning field trips or interviews with experts, encourage students to ask them about the role of collaboration in their work.

As soon as project teams are formed, Erin Brandvold has students draw up team contracts. "They agree on three to five things that they promise to do, such as having all your materials, meeting deadlines, and staying on task. They also come up with their own consequences," she says, if a student lets down the team. Students keep one another honest, sometimes in amusing ways. "I'll see a student in the back of the room doing push-ups and ask what's going on. He'll tell me, 'Oh, I was off task. This is my consequence.'"

Throughout the project, class norms and routines reinforce a culture of collaboration. Reflection prompts and other formative assessment techniques ask students to evaluate team dynamics and make suggestions for improvement. Consider the following tips from PBL veterans.

Figure 4.4   Sample Team Contract

PROJECT TEAM CONTRACT	
Project Name:	
Team Members:	
OUR AGREEMENT	

☐ We all promise to listen to each other's ideas with respect.

☐ We all promise to do our work as best as we can.

☐ We all promise to do our work on time.

☐ We all promise to ask for help if we need it.

☐ We all promise to _____

If someone on our team breaks one or more of our agreements, the team may have a meeting and ask the person to follow our agreement. If the person still breaks the agreements, we will ask our teacher to help find a solution.

Date: _____

Team Member Signatures

_____   _____

_____   _____

_____   _____

Mix up the dynamics: Doing team projects doesn't mean students are always working in the same small groups. Some learning activities, such as Socratic seminars, involve the whole class. Mini-lessons might pull together students from several different teams who need additional instruction or scaffolding. (More about scaffolding is in Chapter 6.) More introverted students will appreciate opportunities to take a break from the social demands of teamwork and work on their own for part of the project.

Start and end project work time with team check-ins: These are opportunities for teams to set goals, report on progress, ask clarifying questions, and remind one another of upcoming deadlines. Making time for teams to regroup, even briefly, reinforces good communication and keeps everyone focused on shared goals.

Reflect on teamwork: At key times during a project, encourage students to reflect on how their team is working together. If collaboration is a key learning goal of the project, make sure you have a rubric or other set of criteria for it, and then use it for reflection prompts. Do all members of the team feel like they have a voice? How does the team show that it welcomes each student's gifts and talents? How could the team get better at collaboration? At the end of the project, have students reflect on how teamwork helped or hindered their results. Based on this experience, how do they want teamwork to go differently next time?

Expand Your Project Management Strategies

By developing a range of project management strategies, you will be better able to track the moving pieces of projects while keeping the focus on learning goals. Be strategic, too, about helping students develop their own tools and strategies for project management. These will serve them well not only in PBL but in life.

Employ tools and routines that help students with the process of learning through projects. Tools such as calendars, team logs, and task trackers help students plan, organize, and recognize their progress. These tools serve a different purpose than rubrics and other assessment tools that get at understanding (and which are also critically important in PBL). Project management tools are about productivity and self-management. They help to clarify what we have accomplished so far, what we need to do next, by when we need to do it, and who's doing what.

A word of caution, though. Emphasizing project management doesn't mean that students are following step-by-step instructions or learning at the same pace. Neither are they left to their own devices to get from start to finish. Instead, project management tools and routines help students stay organized and informed so they can successfully drive more of their own learning. Your tool kit provides an early warning system if projects are getting off track.

Attending to the many pieces of a project can be challenging for students. One project alone generates a substantial amount of "stuff," such as need-to-know questions, curated resources, research notes, journals, and more. To help her math students with organization, Telannia Norfar keeps a project folder on each team's worktable. "I replenish it every week," she says, adding new assignments and calendar updates. Students know they can refer to the folder to find what they need to proceed with the project. Similarly, Rebecca Newburn uses a website to house all the project assignments and curated resources that her middle schoolers may need.

Many PBL teachers create a physical project wall in the classroom to display the driving question, project calendar, need-to-knows, and other components. It's not a static display but instead keeps evolving as the project unfolds.

A digital project center serves the same purpose and has the added advantage of being accessible any time students are online. For parents, a digital project center provides a window into students' learning as it unfolds, along with practical information such as upcoming deadlines, resource needs, field trips, and other logistical details.

In class, students can use the project wall or center to refer to their own need-to-know questions to help them with research. Their list will likely expand as they dig deeper. They can add new questions they want to investigate and cross off questions they have addressed.

By keeping this information accessible, the project wall helps students not only stay organized but also drive more of their own learning.

Project walls are different from traditional bulletin boards; they focus on the learning that's happening *right now*—not as showcases for exemplary final products. They give students ready access to tools and scaffolds for just-in-time learning, and they are as useful for high school students as they are for primary students. (To learn more about how project walls support Project Based Teaching, see the Coaches' Notebook at the end of this chapter.)

Routines offer more tools to reinforce effective project management as part of the classroom culture. As Doug Lemov (2015) reminds us, a classroom routine is "a procedure or system that has become automatic, which students do either without much oversight, without intentional cognition (in other words, as a habit), and/or of their own volition and without teacher prompting (for example, note taking while reading)" (p. 353).

Some routines increase efficiency for regular tasks, such as turning in homework or taking attendance. In PBL, routines can also help students manage their own learning and encourage deeper thinking. Visible Thinking routines, developed by Harvard's Project Zero (n.d.), are used by many PBL teachers. These research-based routines "loosely guide learners' thought processes and encourage active processing. They are short, easy-to-learn mini-strategies that extend and deepen students' thinking and become part of the fabric of everyday classroom life" (para. 3). Although thinking routines are useful for scaffolding inquiry, they also can help students manage more of their own learning by giving them reliable structures for moving forward with their projects.

For example, teacher Raleigh Werberger relied on a routine called See/Think/Wonder throughout an extended interdisciplinary project (which he describes in detail in *From Project-Based Learning to Artistic Thinking: Lessons Learned from Creating an UnHappy Meal* [2015]). The routine encourages close observation and scaffolds inquiry by prompting students to consider three questions: *What do you see? What do you think about that? What does it make you wonder?*

Regular use of See/Think/Wonder inspired curiosity in his student writers throughout the project and also helped them organize their project workflow. As Werberger (2015) explains,

> This format—the introduction of a thinking routine to stimulate observations and questions at the beginning of each new topic, the formulation of an inquiry-based investigation from those observations and questions, and the subsequent rounds of writing, critique, and rewriting—essentially became the working formula for the rest of the school year. (p. 49)

It takes time and effort to establish classroom routines to support PBL, acknowledges Erin Brandvold, "but it's important to spend that time so that students can do thinking and problem solving without you."

To help her students manage more of their own learning, she introduces tools such as graphic organizers to help them with research and checklists to help them remember steps for completing milestone assignments. "You need to make the instructions clear," she adds, "so that you don't have to keep explaining. That allows students to get to the work more quickly." If students ask her a logistical question and she knows the answer is right in front of them on a handout, she may say, "I believe in you. You can figure it out on your own."

Consider what happens when students develop a routine for conducting effective meetings as a way to troubleshoot team challenges. A few simple steps keep the discussion focused on getting to solutions instead of devolving into a gripe session. This routine is used by an elementary teacher to help his students manage teamwork during projects:

1. **What's our agenda?** What's the specific issue, concern, or opportunity we need to talk about? (Hint: Don't hold meetings for the sake of meetings!)
2. **What do we know about this?** Team members have a respectful discussion, inviting all perspectives while keeping the focus on the agenda topic.

3. **What are our next steps?** Have we resolved the issue ourselves, or do we need help from the teacher? Who's going to do what as follow-up?

Establishing a new routine like this takes deliberate practice. You might want to first model a team meeting in a fishbowl or do a role-play to demonstrate good and bad meeting etiquette. When students start to hold their own team meetings, join them as an observer and help them refocus on their agenda if the meeting starts to get off track.

Elementary teachers often use the routine "ask three before me" to encourage students to turn to one another for answers instead of relying on the teacher as the only source of information. A teacher in Memphis, Tennessee, came up with her own version of this routine to help her 9th graders become more confident at managing the process of PBL. Instructional coach Ian Stevenson describes how this routine gradually shifted the culture of this teacher's classroom:

> Her students were new to PBL. They were used to being spoon-fed all the information by their previous teachers. To encourage more self-direction, this teacher didn't want to be the first one students turned to every time they had a question about their project. She introduced this simple routine: If you have a question, first ask someone at your table. If that doesn't help, ask someone at another table. Then pause and try to answer the question yourself, reflecting on the information you have received. If you're still unsure, then come talk to me.

> The teacher quickly realized that a routine like this has to be present in the classroom all the time if it's going to make a difference. She made a poster outlining the three steps and put it up in a prominent place in the classroom. [See Figure 4.5.] During my coaching observations, she asked me to pay attention to how often she referred students to the poster instead of just answering their questions. It took effort on her part not to just give them quick answers. She pushed herself to refer students to the poster and ask, "Where are you in the process?"

Figure 4.5   What to Do When I Feel Confused

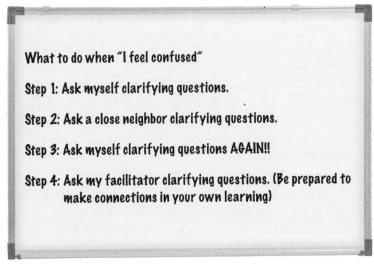

What to do when "I feel confused"

Step 1: Ask myself clarifying questions.

Step 2: Ask a close neighbor clarifying questions.

Step 3: Ask myself clarifying questions AGAIN!!

Step 4: Ask my facilitator clarifying questions. (Be prepared to make connections in your own learning)

Source: Used with permission from Ian Stevenson.

Student response was interesting. At first, there was a lot of grumbling. Some students complained, "You never help us!" But gradually, they realized they could help each other with some of the logistical questions. Once that happened, the teacher started getting deeper questions from students. Their questions for her shifted from logistics to content. As this routine became ingrained, students came to realize that learning can look and sound and mean something different than what they had experienced before. They may have to put in more effort, but it pays off in the end.

Technology Tools for Project Management

Middle school history teacher Tom Neville leverages technology to foster student collaboration in PBL, sometimes across distances. The ongoing Monuments Project (www.monumentsproject.org) involves students from multiple countries to conduct historical research and tell the stories of American veterans from World War I who are buried overseas. To help students manage their learning, he created an online briefcase that links to relevant databases, digital tools, and templates for project management.

Neville's philosophy for integrating technology in PBL is simple. "It is not about the technology or any particular tool but using them at the right time and place," he says. "If we can expose students to some of the best options available and get them to be thoughtful about their choices, it's ultimately more important than being super-skillful with any single one of them."

Which tools belong in your PBL briefcase? Here are some suggestions to consider.

Cloud-based tools for collaboration: G Suite for Education (formerly Google Apps for Education) includes a wide range of cloud-based tools for collaboration, communication, and project management, including a calendar, collaborative documents and forms, and Google Classroom (https://edu.google.com/k-12-solutions/g-suite). Microsoft 365 also includes online tools for content creation, collaboration, and team management.

Digital classroom: Learning management platforms allow teachers to create customized digital classrooms with features to suit specific project needs such as calendars, groups, announcements, grading features, portfolios, and more. Examples include Edmodo (www.edmodo.com) and ClassDojo (www.classdojo.com).

Wikis: Websites that can be easily edited by multiple authors, wikis are useful for creating, sharing, and managing content during projects. Examples include PBworks (www.pbworks.com/education) and Google Sites (https://sites.google.com).

Project trackers: Slack (https://slack.com) and Trello (https://trello.com) are two examples of tools used both within education and by professionals to track the progress of team projects and facilitate collaboration.

Digital bulletin boards: These are useful for formative assessment, brainstorming, and resource sharing. A popular example is Padlet (http://padlet.com).

Making the Most of Learning Time

When we explored strategies for designing and planning high-quality projects in Chapter 2, we discussed the wisdom of starting with the end in mind. That's a reliable way to focus on important learning goals and build academic rigor into your project plan. As part of planning, you also thought about a culminating event with a public audience, sharing of a publication or website, or other demonstration of learning. This gives students not only an authentic audience but also an authentic deadline. Once you launch the project, the countdown to showtime starts ticking. How will you ensure that all students master learning goals by the culmination of the project?

When it comes to managing time, you want to be mindful of the project calendar while also helping students develop their own time-management strategies. Milestone assignments will help students see how even big projects unfold with a series of smaller steps. Giving students realistic but firm deadlines for these milestones will help them learn to meet mini-deadlines and prevent a last-minute crunch.

You also want to keep the calendar flexible and make adjustments based on what's happening with student learning. Telannia Norfar, for example, had planned to have her geometry students go through at least two rounds of practice sessions with their peers before they presented their final home design plans to their client. However, she realized that students needed more time than she had anticipated to grapple with math concepts. She adjusted the calendar accordingly, putting more time into mini-lessons and content review, even though that meant only one round of rehearsals.

Project management tips from PBL veterans will help you make more time for deep learning.

Remove bottlenecks: High school science teacher Brandon Cohen structures projects to include both whole-class and small-group assignments. His goal as a project manager is to be able to step away to work with a few students—perhaps showing them how to use lab equipment or tools—and know that the rest of the class will stay focused on the work at hand. "That takes a culture of trust. It also means students need to know the assignment. What is it? Why are we doing it? What's due when?" One of his management strategies is to make sure he is never a bottleneck to student progress. "If a student needs my attention and I can't give it right then, that student has other avenues. It might be asking for help from a peer or shifting to another task until I am available."

Differentiate as needed: Some students will need additional support or structure as they learn to manage their time and workflow. Address the needs of students with attention disorders and other special needs by helping them chunk project work into manageable pieces, stay focused, and anticipate what's next. Help students develop more independence as learners by acquiring their own strategies for self-management. (For a more detailed discussion of scaffolding in PBL, see Chapter 6.)

Go with the flow: Formative assessment strategies (which will be discussed in detail in Chapter 5) are essential for checking on student understanding throughout the project. But how do you check on productivity without interrupting students' flow? A useful strategy that James Fester discovered when he was teaching middle school is to put a mini-whiteboard on each table and have students jot down a few words to describe what they're working on. He compares this to an approach he's seen in museums where experts put up a sign to tell curious visitors, "Here's what I'm doing today." For the teacher, this approach "makes it easy to eyeball what students are working on and where I might help." He doesn't take credit for the idea, though. "It came from a student who got tired of me interrupting her. One day, she put a sticky note on her table that said, 'I'm doing _____.' I thought, what a brilliant idea!"

Use group work time strategically: When student teams are working productively on projects, use that class time for observations and check-ins. That's the advice of PBL veteran Kevin Gant (2017), who suggests that work time gives teachers opportunities to meet with teams on a rotating basis, observe group collaboration, join small-group conversations, or offer mini-lessons to scaffold learning. "Plan group work time with the question, 'What will I [the teacher] be doing at the same time?' If you don't have a plan," he adds, "your time won't be nearly as well spent" (para. 9).

Don't skimp on reflection: Finding time for reflection can be a challenge during the "busyness" of a project. Resist the temptation to cut this corner. Even a few minutes at the end of a class period can be enough to have students pause and take stock of their learning. Where are they struggling? What's going well in the project? Mix up reflection prompts and methods to avoid rote answers. For example, have students interview one another, share a tweet, or use emojis to reflect on how they're feeling about the project.

Build in breaks: Fatigue can derail progress, especially on longer and more complex projects. That's why Jim Bentley chunks project assignments with his student filmmakers. "During a project work session, we might work on something specific to the project for 45 minutes, and then come back to it later in the day. After doing something intense like script critiques, we might shift gears and work on diagramming sentences for a while. It's nice to have a mental break."

Flip your classroom: In the flipped classroom model, teachers replace in-class lectures with video recordings, which students view as homework. This approach can be used in PBL to create more time for small-group or personalized instruction. Economics teacher Jason Welker, for example, uses video lectures to cover economic content he wants all students to comprehend. (Other teachers might use ready-made videos such as those from Khan Academy.) During class, he meets with each project team to make sure students can apply the big concepts (from the video homework) to their specific project. These small-group discussions tend to go deeper into content than traditional lectures. For an environmental economics project, for example, student teams applied economic theory to address one of the United Nations Sustainable Development Goals. The project led to real action, such as convincing school administrators to invest in a carbon offset project that students had vetted.

Integrate the workshop model: The workshop model, a tried-and-true instructional approach most often used to develop literacy, also supports effective management of learning activities across disciplines in PBL. Ray Ahmed, for example, regularly incorporates a writers' workshop into his high school chemistry class. The workshop approach not only helps students improve their scientific writing but also builds their skills of giving and receiving peer feedback and advocating for the help they need. He explains how this works in a chemistry project: "A student chooses a piece of writing and says, 'Hey, group, I'm ready to share and ask for feedback.' The student who is presenting acknowledges what he or she sees as strengths in the piece of work. Then the student says, 'Here's what I need help with. What are my next steps to make this better?'" Ahmed reminds students that this type of collaboration is exactly how professional scientists improve their work. "If you're working in a chemistry lab," he says, drawing on his own experiences, "you're presenting your work every two weeks. This kind of critique is central to the discipline. It's what scientists do."

In Ahmed's classes, both teacher and peers provide early feedback on student writing. As the project nears completion, external experts come in to provide additional critique. By that point in the project, students have come to appreciate the value of feedback to improve their work. Knowing that they are going to publish their work and present it to a public audience motivates them to strive for professional-quality scientific writing and presentation.

Coaches' Notebook: Capturing Artifacts of Learning

In the Northern California district where James Fester is an instructional coach, teachers have become enthusiastic adopters of strategies to make learning visible. One such strategy is the process wall, which houses artifacts of learning as a project unfolds. (Other teachers may refer to this tool as a project wall or project board.)

To build their walls, Fester's colleagues typically use long pieces of butcher paper they tape up in a prominent spot in the classroom. As the project progresses, they add artifacts of student learning— need-to-know questions, examples of exit tickets, sketch notes, or perhaps entries from reflection journals. "It becomes a running record of the project," Fester explains. "It's not just one form of information. It keeps evolving."

At the end of the project, teachers can roll up the whole thing, saving all that rich information to inform future planning. The next time they want to teach the same project, they can review the artifacts of learning to recall high points and specific challenges. Having a running record of the project will help teachers make modifications, updates, or extensions, improving the project through iteration and reflection.

For students, the wall serves a number of functions. "It's a tool for accountability, assessment, inquiry, scaffolding, and building the classroom culture," Fester says. "If a student has been absent, he or she can quickly catch up. You can go back and revise or add to a previous entry, modeling the importance of revision. When it's time for reflection, students don't have to remember what they did earlier—it's all right there. They can see the scope of the entire project. Most of all, seeing all these examples of student work helps students see themselves in the room. That leads to more buy-in."

Process walls are useful not only for project management but also as coaching tools. Fester explains, "A coach or administrator can walk into a classroom, take a look at the wall, and see at a glance where students are in the project. It gives you the context of what students are learning. An administrator or coach can look at this and also find evidence of Project Based Teaching Practices."

Strategies to Manage Activities: Key Takeaways

In this chapter, you have read about a range of strategies to manage activities in PBL. Perhaps you have not previously thought about yourself as a project manager or considered the self-management skills that students develop through PBL. As you consider these aspects of managing activities, think about the management strategies you need to incorporate:

- **Teamwork:** What's your plan for forming project teams? How do you help teams get off to a strong start? How do you check in on teams and troubleshoot challenges?
- **Tools:** Which of the technology tools described in this chapter are you already using? How might you leverage digital tools to accomplish learning goals in projects?

- **Time:** In planning your project calendar, do you leave enough time in the "messy middle" for students to revise their work based on feedback? When teams are working productively, how are you using class time to observe and check in on learning?

On Your PBL Bookshelf

Never Work Harder Than Your Students and Other Principles of Great Teaching: Veteran educator Robyn R. Jackson guides readers through seven principles of effective teaching that encourage student-centered learning.

PBL for 21st Century Success: This publication from the Buck Institute for Education explains how to help students develop each of the "four Cs"—critical thinking, collaboration, communication, and creativity—through projects that deliberately teach and assess these success skills.

Project Management Toolkit for Teachers: The Project Management Institute Educational Foundation publishes this user-friendly resource for teachers that comes in two versions: one aligned with industry standard terminology, and one aligned with PBL terminology. Project management advice, geared toward ages 10–18, helps prepare students for college and careers.

Reinventing Project Based Learning: Your Field Guide to Real-World Projects in the Digital Age (3rd ed.): Suzie Boss and Jane Krauss connect the dots between effective technology integration and PBL.

Tasks Before Apps: Designing Rigorous Learning in a Tech-Rich Classroom: Monica Burns advocates for focusing on learning goals as a first step in effective technology integration. Plentiful examples show how to use digital tools for creation, curiosity, and collaboration.

5

Assess Student Learning

*Balance formative and summative assessment and
provide students with feedback from multiple sources to help
them achieve deep learning and produce high-quality work in PBL.*

After weeks of working on the designs of their tiny houses, Cheryl Bautista's 3rd graders were ready to make final presentations. Teams took turns sharing their detailed blueprints, scale models, budget calculations, and pitches with their clients. Clients hung on every word and examined every artifact that students had produced in response to their driving question: *Given a budget, how can we as a design team plan a home for a family, taking into consideration space, location, time, labor, materials, and personal preferences?*

What might not have been obvious to the audience was how the feedback, revision, and improvements that had taken place during previous weeks had prepared students for this event. Formative assessment throughout the project included teacher feedback, peer assessment, expert consultation, and self-reflection. All of that shaped students' learning and prepared them to put their best ideas forward for the culminating event.

Why Comprehensive Assessment Is Critical to PBL Success

In PBL, a key factor that makes the difference for student learning is a comprehensive approach to assessment. Assessment in PBL moves students toward mastery. It's not about "gotcha" grades or a means of sorting students by ability levels. As assessment expert Rick Stiggins (2007) suggests, the right kind of assessment puts all students on winning streaks. That's especially true in PBL, where the focus of assessment should be squarely on student growth.

★ Gold Standard Project Based Teaching Practices: Assess Student Learning

A variety of Project Based Teaching strategies contribute to comprehensive assessment. Assessment of different forms and formats takes place from start to finish of a project. Indicators for assessing student learning from the Gold Standard Project Based Teaching Rubric include the following points:

- Project products and other sources of evidence are used to thoroughly assess subject-area standards as well as success skills.

- Individual student learning—not just team-created products—is adequately assessed.

- Formative assessment is used regularly and frequently with a variety of tools and processes.

- Structured protocols for critique and revision are used regularly at checkpoints; students give and receive effective feedback to inform instructional decisions and students' actions.

- Regular, structured opportunities are provided for students to self-assess their progress and, when appropriate, assess peers on their performance.

- Standards-aligned rubrics are used by students and the teacher throughout the project to guide both formative and summative assessment.

See the Appendix for the complete Project Based Teaching Rubric.

📹 A companion video about assessing learning can be found at www.bie.org.

Strategies for Striking a Balance

Many of the assessment tools that will serve you well in PBL—such as quizzes, observations, and protocols for giving feedback—are probably already familiar to you and your students. The shift that happens with Project Based Teaching is to be more strategic about when, why, and how assessment happens.

Formative assessment—assessment *for* learning—needs to occur at frequent intervals throughout a project. Students also need adequate time to revise their work based on feedback, producing multiple drafts of final products as they work toward excellence.

Summative assessment—assessment *of* learning—happens at the end of the project, but students should begin the project with a clear understanding of how they will be assessed. Teachers make their assessment plans transparent when they provide students with a rubric at the start of the project that defines mastery of specific learning goals in student-friendly language. Some teachers prefer to construct the rubric with their students, as teacher Erin Brandvold explains later in this chapter.

Assessment in PBL also strikes a balance between individual and team assessment, self- and peer assessment, and assessment of content mastery and of success skills. It adds up to a multifaceted picture of student learning over time, with students themselves as active participants in the process.

To help you plan for effective assessment, let's take a closer look at four teacher strategies that help put students on a winning streak in PBL: be transparent about criteria for success, emphasize formative assessment, balance individual and team assessment, and encourage feedback from multiple sources.

Be Transparent About Criteria for Success

When Rebecca Newburn was planning a project about climate change, she knew she wanted her middle school students to come away with two enduring understandings: how humans affect Earth's climate, and what humans can do to mitigate climate change.

Those learning goals align with the Next Generation Science Standards and Common Core State Standards, making them a good fit for an in-depth inquiry project. They also reflect Newburn's desire to help students make personal connections to science and work toward solutions. "When planning a project, I think, how does this content relate to students' lives? After they learn about this, how can they feel empowered to make a difference?"

Newburn makes those goals transparent to students in a number of ways, starting with the driving question. At the start of the project she called Face, Place, Story: The Science and Stories of Climate Change, Newburn's driving question pointed to the applied learning ahead: *How are different communities affected by climate change, and what can we do to make a positive change?* Throughout the project, the learning activities, student research, expert consultations, fieldwork, and reflections all connected back to that driving question, which helped students stay focused on the learning goals and prepare to take action.

At each stage of the project, students understood the criteria for success, which were clearly spelled out on Newburn's class website. The teacher informed students in advance of milestone assignments and deadlines. They also understood that, by the end of the project, they would need to apply their understanding and propose a climate change action plan that would have a real impact. By providing students with the big picture of the project and assessing and guiding their learning along the way, Newburn was setting up her students for success.

As the project was coming to a close, Newburn joined a team of students for a critical review of their climate change action plan. They had chosen to create a video campaign to reduce food waste. "They explained why this is such an important issue. They had good data," she said, and they presented their arguments using academic vocabulary. They cited sources. Newburn suggested a few minor edits to improve the production but had only positive feedback about students' understanding of key concepts.

"They understood that reducing food waste is something that they as kids can do to make a real difference. That was exciting," and it shows what students can accomplish when they tackle a goal that matters to them. To make sure your students understand—and buy into—the learning goals of PBL, share your assessment plan with them soon after the entry event.

Unpack the rubric: Depending on your PBL experience and school context, you may be creating a project rubric from scratch, repurposing one you have used in the past, or using a common rubric that is shared across your grade level or school system. Whatever the source, make sure that students understand the assessment language and know how to use the rubric to guide their growth as learners.

In a social studies project with her 4th graders, for example, Abby Schneiderjohn used the same rubric for evaluating essays that students were already familiar with from writers' workshop. Students were able to use the rubric to revise their rough drafts and critique one another's writing during peer reviews.

With her high school world history classes, Erin Brandvold guided students through a process of creating a scoring guide to assess their mock trial performance at the end of their revolutions project. She explains how that came together:

> After students had time to watch and analyze film clips of trials and practice their own court arguments, we used a protocol to come up with their criteria for effective participation in a mock trial. To reach consensus, we used a protocol called GOILS: Groups of Increasingly Larger Size. Students first work individually to come up with five criteria on their own. Then they compare criteria with a partner, and together they decide on a list of five criteria. Pairs then meet in groups of four, and they do the same thing. That process continues, with groups doubling in size each time until the whole class comes to agreement. Students' five criteria [listing specific bullet points about evidence, argumentation, presentation

skills, legal professionalism, and knowledge] were what the jury used during the mock trial to evaluate their courtroom performance.

Cocreating rubrics reinforces a classroom culture of excellence. Brandvold says, "The process encourages students to think, 'If I were to do this really well, what would that look like?'" Students have a better understanding of high-quality work by generating their own indicators for the learning goals that the teacher has identified.

If students are new to using rubrics, build time into the early days of your project calendar for them to unpack the language and practice using the assessment tool. One helpful strategy is to share samples of student work from a previous project and have students assess the quality, using the rubric as their scoring guide. Make sure students understand the assessment vocabulary. Help them define any unfamiliar terms, or suggest synonyms they do understand.

Chemistry teacher Ray Ahmed introduces students to their rubric at the beginning of the school year. He explains that the rubric, created by the New York Performance Standards Consortium, will be used for summative assessment of their second-semester projects. This will be a high-stakes assessment, and results will count toward students' graduation requirements.

Instead of just handing out the rubric for future reference, Ahmed starts using it with students right away as a learning tool. They look at the rubric next to a scientific article. "This is where we're headed," the teacher explains. "We're doing the work of scientists." As part of the project, students will write their own articles about the experiments they design. With that end in mind, they read the journal article together, analyzing it as an exemplar by looking at the criteria called for in the rubric. This creates opportunities for students to ask questions and start thinking about what is required to produce high-quality work.

To help students focus on a specific learning goal, you can show them just one row from a rubric. Figure 5.1, for example, shows the row for "Contextualize" from the rubric that Ahmed uses with his students. If you were sharing this with your students, you would want to make sure they understood key vocabulary, including *original sources*, *appropriately cited*, and *hypothesis/theses*. You would help them see that the language is parallel as you read from left to right, but the modifiers change as the quality of work changes. A key takeaway for students is for them to see how the learning path leads to proficiency—and beyond.

Figure 5.1   Criteria for Excellence

Performance Indicator	Outstanding	Good	Competent	Needs Revision
Contextualize	Background research has been thoroughly conducted using at least two original sources. Sources are all appropriately cited. The significance of the problem is clearly stated. The hypotheses/theses are grounded in the background research.	Background research has been thoroughly conducted. Sources are appropriately cited. The significance of the problem is stated. The hypotheses/theses are relevant to the background research.	Background research is included in the introduction. Sources are cited. The significance of the problem is stated. The hypotheses/theses are clearly stated.	Background research is not included in the introduction. Sources are not cited. The significance of the problem is not stated. The hypotheses/theses are not stated.

Source: From New York Performance Standards Consortium. Available at www.performanceassessment.org/rubrics.

If success skills, such as collaboration or critical thinking, are going to be assessed as part of the project, then make sure those learning goals are also clearly defined. The Buck Institute for Education recommends using one rubric for assessing content knowledge/ final product and a second rubric for assessing the success skills specifically targeted as project learning goals. (Rubrics for assessing the four Cs are available to download at bie.org.)

Once you're sure that students understand the rubric, encourage them to use it to guide their learning throughout the project. In

Telannia Norfar's math classroom, for example, she keeps a folder on each table with all the relevant project documents, including the rubric. While students are working on problem-solving tasks related to the project, she circulates and makes notes on mailing labels.

"I walk, listen, assess, and then stick notes on their desks about what they've done well. They have the rubric right in front of them. They can look at my feedback, and then we can talk about what they need to do next to improve." One student, for example, wondered why he wasn't getting better feedback on his work even though he was arriving at correct answers. "I told him to look at the rubric. He said, 'Oh! I didn't explain how I solved the problem.' The next time, he explained his solution all over the place." He understood that the goal wasn't simply to check the box but to produce high-quality work.

❍ Try This: Assess 21st Century Success Skills

Most teachers are used to assessing content knowledge and skills. During a project, you can use quizzes, tests, writing assignments, and other traditional tools for this purpose—and you can find evidence in the products students create and the presentations they make. To assess success skills, such as critical thinking/problem solving, collaboration, and creativity/innovation, you can use tools and strategies such as the following ideas:

- Share a rubric or another set of criteria with students (or co-create one) that describes what the specific success skill looks like. Examples can be found at www.bie.org/objects/cat/rubrics.

- Observe students as they work on a project, and make notes on how they are demonstrating the use of one or more success skills. Create a checklist of observable behaviors, drawing from the rubric or other set of criteria.

- Meet with individual students or with teams during a project to discuss how they are building competence in one or more success skills.

> **⊙ Try This: Assess 21st Century Success Skills (*continued*)**
>
> • Have students self-assess their use of the success skill, refer-ring to the rubric or other set of criteria during a project and at the end as a summative assessment. During and at the end of a project, ask students to assess how well they and their peers used one or more success skills (especially collaboration).
>
> • Have students keep a journal during a project in which they document their use of one or more success skills, and use it at the end of the project to reflect on what they gained.
>
> • Ask questions during student presentations (or encourage their audience to ask questions) that uncover their use of success skills. For example, ask them to describe the process they used to solve a problem or develop an innovative product.

Emphasize Formative Assessment

Visit a PBL classroom and you will see formative assessment taking place in a variety of ways—exit tickets that allow teachers to check on student understanding at the end of a class period, reflec-tion journals in which students assess their own learning, protocols such as gallery walks that help peers offer one another specific feed-back, and more.

A word of caution is necessary, though. Increasing the fre-quency of your formative assessment checks does not mean putting more emphasis on grading. Grades can feel like stop signs to stu-dents, signaling that an assignment is over and done with. Formative assessment, by contrast, is all about what comes next in the learning experience.

For Project Based Teachers, formative assessment provides diagnosis and information to plan their next teaching moves. Do they need to teach a concept in a different way? Provide additional resources? Challenge students to go deeper or extend their thinking? For students, formative assessment provides just-in-time feedback to support learning and help them produce high-quality products that demonstrate their understanding. Rather than assigning points or scores for every instance of formative assessment, reserve grades for major milestone assignments and summative assessment.

Teacher Jim Bentley wisely emphasizes formative assessment throughout projects. "If feedback is only given at the end of a project," he cautions, "it's already too late." With his 6th graders, Bentley uses a combination of technology tools, critique protocols, and teacher observations to check on their understanding. He might ask a content-related question in Google Classroom or post a prompt on an electronic bulletin board called Padlet. Students' responses tell him if anyone's stuck or struggling so he can plan small-group instruction or individual attention. He schedules gallery walks to elicit peer critique of works-in-progress, scaffolding feedback by encouraging students to consider these questions: *What's working? What's confusing? What was something you wondered?*

Often, Bentley adds, effective formative assessment is simply pulling up a chair and watching and listening as students tackle a learning activity. If they get stuck or seem ready to go deeper, he offers prompts or clues. Each instance of formative assessment is another opportunity to provide students with feedback that is timely, understandable, and actionable (Fisher, Frey, & Hite, 2016).

Similar assessment practices guide the learning in Rebecca Newburn's science classroom. While her students were working on their climate change project, she employed a variety of formative assessment techniques to check their understanding and adjust instruction as needed. Some moves were planned in advance; others happened in the moment.

Assess prior knowledge: To launch the project and assess students' prior knowledge, Newburn asked students to do a quick-write explaining the difference between *climate* and *weather*. To make the assignment more engaging, she modeled the assignment on Twitter. Instead of actually using Twitter, however, students produced "paper tweets," and each post was limited to a specific number of characters.

To challenge their initial thinking, Newburn next gave students 10-day weather forecasts for three cities from different regions (Alaska, Oregon, and Florida). Could students tell which was which? Were the forecasts consistent with what they expected? How did the forecasts cause students to revise their definition of weather versus climate?

Next, students read their definitions to tablemates and received Twitter-style responses. If partners disagreed, they would reply and explain in a new paper tweet what wasn't accurate. If they thought it was good, they would "like" the tweet. And if they thought it was good enough to share, they would retweet the definition. The fast-paced activity not only gave the teacher insights into prior knowledge but also signaled to students that Newburn wouldn't be the only one giving feedback during the project.

Give milestone assignments: To make sure students understood the science of climate change—specifically the effect it can have on human populations—Newburn gave a milestone assignment she had planned for a couple weeks into the project, after students had time to build their content understanding. Working in small teams (based on their choice of geographic locations), students were assigned to produce a poster that "dissected a disaster" for a community somewhere in the world that is vulnerable to climate change.

The assignment provided a way for Newburn to check content understanding before students moved ahead with the development of their action plans. She wanted to know, "Do they know what causes severe weather events? Do they understand how climate change is going to affect weather? Can they make predictions (such as flooding or drought conditions)? Can they put a human face on that story and also back it up with data?"

Built into the poster assignment were opportunities for peer assessment. Student teams began with rough sketches of their posters. They presented them to classmates for initial feedback about content (with the teacher listening to address any misunderstandings).

Once they were clear on the content, they were ready to move on to designing full-size posters, which they presented jigsaw-style to the other teams. As part of her assessment, Newburn listened to make sure every student on each team was able to accurately explain the content.

Observe and question: Along with planned assessment such as the disaster posters, Newburn allowed herself ample time to be an informal observer throughout the project.

Effective formative assessment "is all about the questions," she says. When students are having discussions about their learning, she'll listen, ask probing questions, "and then step back and let kids have the conversation. I'm not exactly a fly on the wall, but I'll only step in if I hear something that needs to be revisited or is a misconception."

Some of her favorite formative prompts are generic enough to use again and again. For example: *Can you tell me more about that? Can you give an example? Why do you think that? I want to hear more of your thinking behind what you're saying.* Some prompts reinforce the academic language she wants to hear in the science classroom, such as *What's your claim? How does that evidence support your reasoning?*

With her high school math students, Telannia Norfar uses informal assessment to encourage persistence in students who are struggling. Instead of jumping to their rescue, she says, "I let them know it's OK to run into roadblocks. I might let them wrestle with a problem for a day or two. I'll tell them, 'There's nothing wrong with being stuck. Breathe, and then try approaching the problem in a different way. I'm here for you.'" If the struggle continues, that's the teacher's signal to offer additional instruction or teach a concept in a different way.

Norfar's approach to assessment is consistent with the classroom culture. "We talk about the value of failing forward," she says, to encourage risk taking and foster a growth mindset. "Persistence in math is hard," she acknowledges, but the right approach to assessment helps build the mental muscle to keep going.

> **⊘ Try This: Map Your Formative Assessment Strategy**
>
> To plan the formative assessment and checkpoints you will use during a project to ensure students are learning what they need to and are on track toward completing project products, use a Project Assessment Map. You can find a blank form and see completed examples at www.bie.org/object/document/project_assessment_map.
>
> Here's the basic process:
>
> 1. On the left side of the map, list one of the major final products for the project (which serves as a summative assessment).
>
> 2. To the right of the product, list the key knowledge, understanding, and success skills students will need in order to create the product. (These can be expressed as learning goals or targets derived from standards.)
>
> 3. To the right of the outcomes/learning targets, list the formative assessment tools and strategies that will be needed to check student progress toward the learning goals.
>
> Figure 5.2 shows an example from Erin Brandvold's world history project on revolutions.

Balance Individual and Team Assessment

Teamwork is important in PBL, reflecting the important role that collaboration plays in the world beyond the classroom. That's why Project Based Teachers consider team dynamics during project planning. They build a collaborative classroom culture in which every student feels safe and where every voice matters. They foster effective collaboration while managing, scaffolding, and coaching learning. Not surprisingly, teamwork also plays an important role in assessment.

The question that perplexes many newcomers to PBL is this: How are you supposed to assess individual learning while evaluating something produced by a team? Some students (and also parents) are quick to raise fairness issues if projects are assigned to teams. Some schools have grading policies that make it challenging, at best, to assess team efforts.

Veteran PBL teachers who have navigated this terrain have developed practical strategies to balance individual and team assessments. Here are some of their go-to strategies.

Figure 5.2   Project Assessment Map for the Revolutions on Trial Project

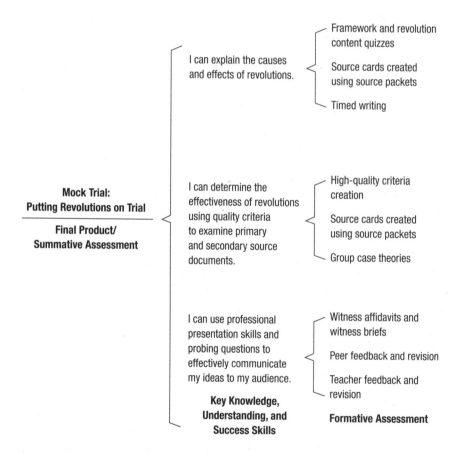

Source: Used with permission from Erin Brandvold.

Clarify which is which: At the project planning stage, decide which assignments will be done individually and which will be done by teams, and then assess accordingly. For example, each student might have to write an essay or take a test to demonstrate understanding of key content. Team products would then require students to apply their understanding to generate a shared solution or product.

In Cheryl Bautista's tiny house project, for example, students were evaluated individually on writing assignments. They wrote opinion pieces about their proposed blueprints, and they all wrote how-to paragraphs about the math concepts that applied to their house design. Team assessments focused only on their presentations to clients.

Like most PBL teachers, Erin Brandvold typically gives individual assignments more weight than team tasks. For the revolutions project, major individual milestones included a timed writing assignment at the end of the third week. That allowed Brandvold to check for content understanding and ascertain whether each student understood how to construct an argument. In the same project, students were assessed as a team on their case theory, which was essentially an outline of their team's trial argument, evidence, and courtroom roles. "That was the only assignment they all got the same grade for," she said. Her intent was to make sure team members were all on the same page and that they all knew the arguments and evidence before preparing for their individual roles during the trial.

Reinforce peer accountability: Assessment strategies help hold students responsible to their teams and avoid the problem of free-riding (or what students sometimes call "slacking") by team members who don't pull their weight. In earlier discussions about managing learning, you read about the use of team contracts to encourage effective teamwork. Some teachers also ask students to assess everyone's contribution to the team as a strategy to reinforce accountability.

Rebecca Newburn, for example, surveys students near the end of a project and asks them to adjust points based on individual effort. If all team members contributed, then the points are shared evenly. "But if someone didn't do their part or someone else did extra work, here's a chance to adjust up or down," she explains. "Because students know this ahead of time, it builds in accountability to the team."

Erin Brandvold schedules opportunities during a project for team members to assess one another on their collaboration skills. "They have to come up with a grade for each team member and explain why," she explains. "I encourage them to be honest. If you've given a high grade [for collaboration] to someone who doesn't deserve it, you're giving that person permission to not contribute to your group." Students also do a final team assessment at the end of the project. Those scores are factored into the collaboration portion of their grade.

Encourage reflection about teamwork: As a formative assessment strategy, ask students to reflect on how well their teams are working together. This might be a journal prompt, question for an exit ticket, or something to bring up when meeting with individual teams. Finding out about team challenges early allows you to help students work out their differences while there's still time to course correct.

Encourage Feedback from Multiple Sources

Unlike traditional assessment, which typically comes only from the teacher, assessment in PBL may come from multiple sources. That includes peers, audiences, and experts, in addition to self-assessment.

Solicit peer feedback: One of the strategies common among Project Based Teachers is the development of a critique culture. That means teaching, modeling, and coaching students how to give and receive peer feedback. Many teachers share the wisdom of PBL expert Ron Berger, who encourages feedback—at all ages—that is kind, specific, and helpful (Berger, Rugan, & Woodfin, 2014). (Watch Berger tell the story of Austin's Butterfly in this video from EL Education: http://modelsofexcellence.eleducation.org/resources/austins-butterfly.)

Erin Brandvold teaches her students to use a variety of protocols for peer feedback. In the revolutions project, for example, teams practiced their courtroom arguments using a fishbowl. One team practiced in the center of the fishbowl, while another team watched and listened in an outer circle. After the observers provided feedback, teams switched positions. After the protocol, both teams had time to make revisions based on feedback.

To ensure that their feedback was specific, Brandvold gave students a graphic organizer to capture observations. In the center column were listed the criteria that students generated as a whole class. In a column on the left, listeners were prompted to make suggestions for improvement: "You didn't do this. Here's what you could have done." On the right, there was space to highlight positives: "You did this. Here's something you should keep doing." The critique experience turned out to be equally useful for performers and listeners. "That was one of the most useful protocols we used in this project," the teacher says.

Invite feedback from audiences: Having an authentic audience for student work increases engagement and encourages students to produce high-quality work. That's why a public product is considered to be an essential element for PBL design. Take advantage of public presentations not just to share project results but also to solicit audience feedback.

Audiences may need coaching from you about how to respond to student work. We heard earlier, for example, how Cheryl Bautista's students presented their tiny house designs to clients as a culminating event. In advance, the teacher provided clients with scoring rubrics and questions to ask students. She also asked clients to choose a favorite design—one that would best suit each client's family. Earlier in the project, students had interviewed clients about their housing needs, design preferences, and more. How well did their designs reflect clients' wishes?

As each student team left the conference room, Bautista watched clients wrestle with their decision. As part of their feedback, clients were asked to provide students with a written explanation of their final choice. Bautista wanted students to hear their reasoning and be able to reflect on that. "Why did they choose one design over another? What made the difference?"

As part of your preparation for public presentations, think about how you will help the audience get ready to actively engage with students. Encourage follow-up questions or audience voting, if appropriate. A high school marketing project, for example, concluded with students pitching their product ideas to an audience of 4th graders.

Teacher Brian Schoch arranged for 4th graders to cast ballots after they had a chance to hear the pitches. Votes didn't factor into grades but still provided meaningful feedback to the high school students.

Similarly, when Brandvold's students rested their case in the revolutions project, the jury came back with a verdict. To reach their decision, jurors relied on the criteria that students had generated. Brandvold also provided jurors with graphic organizers to track evidence presented during the mock trial.

Encourage expert feedback: Many projects include the participation of content experts. Experts may get involved during the research phase or while students are designing and refining products or solutions. Encourage formative feedback from experts who are knowledgeable about the standards of excellence in their disciplines. Experts can also contribute to summative assessment by scoring students on their final presentations or products.

For the tiny house project, Cheryl Bautista's students had multiple opportunities to consult with an engineer. Early in the project, he shared examples of blueprints from projects he had worked on. Later, when students were working on their own blueprints, he encouraged them to make sure drawings were precise, neat, and appropriately labeled. Hearing that feedback from an expert "means more to students than if I told them to keep the lines straight," Bautista says. "When it comes from an expert, it has more weight. It's real."

Ray Ahmed brings in experts to provide feedback on specific aspects of his students' chemistry projects. For a project that involved considerable data gathering about water quality, he enlisted experts in statistics to help students think through how to analyze and present their data. The visitors were diverse, ranging from students who had previously taken the class with Ahmed, to graduate students, to math teachers, to people who use statistics in their work. "It was important to have my students see people who look like them, who are friendly, and who are experts in the work."

Ahmed is also intentional about how students engage with experts. He wants students to set the agenda for their one-to-one conversations with experts. To prepare for a conference, students think through what they want to learn. For example, a student might go through this line of thought: "I'm going to meet with an expert about statistics. I want to learn how to use T-tests. I've done two things about T-tests: I've watched a video, and I've done some practice problems. I still don't get it. Here are two other things I'm thinking about doing." This becomes the basis of the conversation with the expert. "This structure promotes a sense of agency," Ahmed adds, with students advocating for what they need to learn or understand more deeply.

Similarly, Kimberly Head-Trotter invited an expert panel to give feedback to her students when they were near the end of their March on Nashville project. The experts—including a historian and a local citizen involved in social justice efforts—were not the final audience; that was going to be the general public. Their experts' critique inspired students to make a final round of improvements, and their enthusiasm kept students' passion for the project burning bright.

Finally, Assessment of Learning

Education professor Robert Stake is credited with this widely quoted distinction between formative and summative assessment: "When the cook tastes the soup, that's formative; when the guests taste the soup, that's summative" (Scriven, 1991, p. 169).

In PBL, the culmination of a project is when the focus of assessment shifts from assessment for learning (formative) to assessment of learning (summative). To determine whether students have reached the goals set out in the beginning of the project, teachers need to take a critical look at evidence of learning to evaluate what students know or can do as a result of their learning experience.

Summative assessment in PBL can take a variety of forms, depending on the nature of the project. For example, teachers may base their final assessment on

- A score of the final product against the project rubric.
- A performance task to evaluate whether students can apply what they have learned.
- A final exam or major essay that shows how well students understand content.

- Input from experts about students' final presentations or exhibitions of work.
- Student journals, design notebooks, lab reports, or other written products that provide evidence of what students have learned.

Earlier in this chapter, we discussed strategies for balancing individual and team assessment. When it comes to summative assessment, you want to know how much progress each student has made toward meeting learning goals. At the end of a project in which her students acted as financial planners for real-life clients, for example, teacher Telannia Norfar wanted to know how well each student understood the math concepts. Even though students collaborated to make team presentations to their clients, they first worked individually on specific mathematical calculations (such as how to save for a mortgage or pay for college costs). Norfar looked at those calculations to assess content mastery.

◉ Try This: Consider Various Grading Strategies in PBL

Teachers who are new to PBL often wonder about how to assign grades in a project when students work in teams, create authentic products, and focus on success skills in addition to content knowledge. The use of PBL causes many teachers, schools, and districts to rethink assessment and reporting practices. Nevertheless, they have found PBL to be compatible with both traditional and new assessment and reporting practices, including standards- or competency-based grading.

There is no simple recipe for grading in PBL, since every teacher typically has his or her own system and beliefs about it, but here are some ideas from PBL teachers to consider:

- Do not give one grade or number of points for the entire project. Rather, grade smaller assignments, quizzes and other assessments, and deliverables at checkpoints during the project.

> **⊖ Try This: Consider Various Grading Strategies in PBL (*continued*)**
>
> - Base grades mostly on individual performance, not team-created work.
>
> - Consider not grading team-created products at all, since students should still be motivated to do high-quality work by an authentic project that makes their work public.
>
> - Separate grades based on acquisition of content knowledge and skills from the assessment (and possibly grading) of success skills.
>
> - Do not assign grades or points for the *quality* of works-in-progress or drafts; assign points for the *completion* of project deliverables.

Coaches' Notebook: Formative Brainstorm

When teachers first learn about the importance of formative assessment for successful Project Based Learning, they can feel overwhelmed. They may wonder how they will ever come up with enough tools and strategies to keep learning on track. Whether they realize it or not, however, most teachers already have a handy tool kit for formative assessment. In fact, they use check-ins, observations, quizzes, and questioning strategies so often to support learners that they may not recognize what they're doing as formative assessment. It's just good teaching.

Here's a fast-paced coaching activity (modeled on the game Scattergories) to use with a group of teachers. The goal is to help them recognize their own wisdom as formative assessors and also consider creative assessment ideas for PBL:

1. Have teachers form teams of three or four.
2. Explain that they will have five minutes to brainstorm as many formative assessment ideas as they can. Check for

understanding by asking a volunteer to share an example of a formative assessment tool or strategy (e.g., exit ticket, thumbs up/thumbs down).

3. Start the timer.
4. When time's up, have teams report the total number of ideas they generated.
5. Next, have teams take turns sharing out their ideas. Do this "Scattergories" style. That means other teams chime in ("We've got that, too!") if they hear ideas they also came up with. Once duplicates are identified, they get crossed off every team's list.
6. At the end, you will be left with a list of unique ideas for formative assessment. Reflect as a whole group about how and when each of these ideas would be useful to support student learning during PBL.

Strategies to Assess Student Learning: Key Takeaways

In this chapter, you read about many resources to support effective assessment in PBL, along with examples of assessment in action. Take time to reflect on your current practices as you consider strategies to improve your approach to PBL assessment.

- Do your students understand the criteria for assessment? Are you using rubrics to support their growth and reinforce a culture of excellence?
- Does your assessment planning put enough emphasis on formative strategies? Which of the many formative assessment approaches in this chapter will you introduce with your students? What will you hope to learn as a result?
- What's your plan for balancing team and individual assessments? How do you help team members hold one another accountable? If students are producing team products, how will you assess the learning of each student?

- Who provides feedback to your students on their projects? How might you improve the quality of feedback they receive from peers, experts, and public audiences?

On Your PBL Bookshelf

The Formative Assessment Action Plan: Practical Steps to More Successful Teaching and Learning: Assessment experts Douglas Fisher and Nancy Frey show how to engage students as partners in learning through ongoing cycles of formative feedback.

How to Create and Use Rubrics for Formative Assessment and Grading: Susan Brookhart clarifies the purpose and qualities of effective rubrics, showing how these tools are useful for both formative and summative assessment.

An Introduction to Student-Involved Assessment FOR Learning: Jan Chappuis and Rick Stiggins explain how assessment can be a powerful learning tool in this comprehensive book that clarifies everything from learning targets to performance tasks to student portfolios.

Leaders of Their Own Learning: Transforming Schools Through Student-Engaged Assessment: Ron Berger, Leah Rugan, and Libby Woodfin explain how to use student-led assessment to foster academic growth and engage students and families in learning.

Peer Feedback in the Classroom: Empowering Students to Be the Experts: Veteran teacher Starr Sackstein recommends peer feedback strategies to drive learning in a student-centered classroom.

Rigorous PBL by Design: Three Shifts for Developing Confident and Competent Learners: Michael McDowell blends first-person experiences in the PBL classroom with research-based recommendations to increase academic rigor of projects. Building on the work of John Hattie, McDowell shows how to help students move from surface to deep to transfer learning.

6

Scaffold Student Learning

Create conditions so that every student—regardless of prior learning experiences, language fluency, or reading levels—can succeed in PBL.

When Abby Schneiderjohn and her teaching partner redesigned a 4th grade social studies and language arts unit, their goal was to do more than deliver a quick recap of state history. "When students leave fourth grade, most will only remember the Gold Rush and maybe the California missions," the teacher says. "We wanted to go deeper."

That was the genesis of the Great California Adventure project. For eight weeks, students worked in teams to investigate this driving question: *What makes California the Golden State?* Students were asked to select one "golden" episode from history, defend their choice in an essay, and then perform an original skit to bring their example to life.

For the culminating event, the plan called for teams to act out their historical skits before a live audience during a schoolwide exhibition night. Preparing for that grand finale involved a number of milestone assignments, including interviews and other research, persuasive writing, set design, script writing, and public speaking.

Schneiderjohn knew before the project began that her 28 students came with a wide range of backgrounds. Some were California natives; others were recent immigrants to the United States. Some were reading at or above grade level; others were still developing fluency in English. As a class, they had developed a shared understanding of state history through previous literacy units focusing on Native Americans, early explorers, and the Gold Rush. The Great California Adventure project would challenge everyone to think more analytically about history.

To help all learners succeed, the teachers included a number of instructional supports in their project plan. They also introduced just-in-time scaffolds if they saw students struggling.

"It was a balance of what we anticipated and what students needed in the moment," Schneiderjohn explains.

In Project Based Teaching, scaffolding provides the necessary supports so all students can grow as learners, regardless of where they start. Teachers consider everything from how students will access content to their readiness to conduct research and collaborate with teammates. Some scaffolds serve all learners; other supports are tailored to small groups or individual needs. Some scaffolds are planned in advance; others are used as needed. For teachers, getting comfortable with scaffolding means "being able to look at students' work, identify their needs, and then have the tools to intervene as needed," Schneiderjohn says.

■◀ A companion video about scaffolding student learning can be found at www.bie.org.

Why Is Scaffolding Student Learning Essential for PBL?

Scaffolding learning is an important teaching practice generally, but it is critical to helping all students succeed in PBL. The goal is to create conditions and supports so that every student can stretch to reach learning targets. That includes academic goals and success skills. As students develop the competence and confidence to succeed on their own, scaffolds are gradually withdrawn.

Scaffolds enable students to make gains they might not otherwise be able to make (Tomlinson, 2017; Wood, Bruner, & Ross, 1976). As Carol Ann Tomlinson, an authority on differentiated instruction, explains,

> In a differentiated classroom, it's the teacher's goal to figure out where a student is in relation to key learning goals and then provide learning experiences that will push the learner a little further and faster than is comfortable. The teacher coaches for student effort and productive learning choices, and will ensure that there is support necessary to assist the student in reaching the goal that seemed a bit out of reach. (2017, p. 45)

In an equitable classroom, students' prior learning experiences, language fluency, or reading levels are not barriers to success. "Remember that everyone's next step will not be identical and that every student needs scaffolding in order to stretch," advises Tomlinson (2017, p. 45).

That's as true for struggling learners as it is for more academically advanced or gifted students. "It's very easy to fall into the pattern of giving some kids no-brainer tasks and giving other kids the teacher's pet tasks," she cautions. "What you really want is every student to be focused on the essential knowledge, understanding, and skill. And for every student to have to think to do their work" (Tomlinson, quoted in Rebora, 2008, para. 9).

Scaffolding may sound complex, but it doesn't have to be. If you've ever watched a child learn to ride a bike with training wheels, you have witnessed scaffolding in action. The training wheels aren't permanent; they come off when the child is able to balance, steer, and brake. Eventually, after some wobbling and perhaps a few falls, the child is able to ride confidently and independently on two wheels. Similarly, when scaffolding is properly administered in the classroom, it serves as an enabler—not as a disabler (Benson, 1997).

With appropriate scaffolding in place, PBL can be an appropriate and accessible way to learn for students of diverse abilities. However, we can't expect PBL to be a silver bullet. Students who are far behind grade level or who have large gaps of understanding will need targeted attention to build skills and fill knowledge gaps as projects progress. As you will see in the following examples, Project Based Teachers employ a variety of strategies—many of which are also used in more traditional instruction—to ensure that all students make progress toward learning goals.

★ **Gold Standard Project Based Teaching Practices: Scaffold Student Learning**

In a PBL classroom where the teacher is attending to scaffolding, all students have the support they need to succeed. Indicators for Scaffold Student Learning from the Project Based Teaching Rubric include the following points:

- Each student receives necessary instructional supports to access content, skills, and resources; these supports are removed when no longer needed.

- Scaffolding is guided as much as possible by students' questions and needs; the teacher does not front-load too much information at the start of the project but waits until it is needed or requested by students.

- Key success skills are taught using a variety of tools and strategies; students are provided with opportunities to practice and apply them, and then reflect on progress.

- Student inquiry is facilitated and scaffolded, while allowing students to act and think as independently as possible.

See the Appendix for the complete Project Based Teaching Rubric.

Scaffolding the Great California Adventure

Scaffolding the learning in PBL offers an opportunity to tap into familiar instructional strategies. Many of the supports you have used in more traditional lessons—graphic organizers, leveled readers, discussion protocols—will also work well during projects. Using scaffolds effectively in PBL requires getting specific about the learning challenge at hand. Is your goal to support students' mastery of content? To help students develop disciplinary thinking? To scaffold collaboration or other success skills? To develop students' project management strategies? Different scaffolds will serve different purposes. To see what this looks like in action, let's take a closer look at the scaffolding that supported student learning in Abby Schneiderjohn's Great California Adventure project.

Early in the project, when it was time to assign teams, Schneiderjohn and her teaching partner took into account students' research and literacy skills and scaffolded content accordingly. "For our most struggling students, we put them in the team focusing on the Gold Rush because they already had some prior knowledge of that content," she explains. The whole class had studied the Gold Rush in a previous unit, using a guided language program adopted by the district. With that background knowledge of content, students who needed extra support could focus more on writing and less on research.

Another group of students wanted to investigate the history of the Golden Gate Bridge. "We hadn't learned anything about that content yet," Schneiderjohn realized. "They would have to do all the research on their own." Researching the history and engineering of the Golden Gate Bridge seemed like a good stretch for students who had the literacy, language, and research skills to tackle new content on their own.

As the project progressed, the teachers introduced additional scaffolds as needed to help students master specific learning goals. When it came to writing persuasive essays, for example, some students needed more support than others. "We provided a frame that some students used [to organize their writing]; others didn't need it." The teachers also realized that writing a script from a specific character's point of view was a new challenge for nearly all students. "We did a lot of modeling for the whole class about what it means to take a point of view," Schneiderjohn says.

When students were working on their writing assignments, the teachers were deliberate about improving the quality of peer feedback. From their previous experience with the writers' workshop model, students had learned sentence stems for offering feedback (e.g., I like…, I wish…, What if…). "But we still had to scaffold how to give specific feedback," Schneiderjohn says. "We would say, 'In this round of feedback, we're not going to focus on the backdrops or props. Right now, we're only focusing on improving the scripts.' In a later round, feedback was only about acting. How was their performance? How could they improve their body language, voice, or eye contact?" Prompting students to give more focused feedback helped them all put their best work forward when it was showtime.

The teacher moves associated with scaffolding learning happen throughout a project. Some supports are planned in advance; others will be pulled out when students need help to make progress in the project. Some scaffolds will be appropriate for the whole class. Based on formative assessment, you may recognize that some students will require more individualized or small-group support to address specific learning issues. From the teacher's perspective, effective scaffolding starts with a positive teacher mindset: "Let's assume students can all do good work, and let's attend to the ways that they need us to teach them in order to get there" (Tomlinson, quoted in Rebora, 2008, para. 9).

❯ Try This: Plan Scaffolding with a Student Learning Guide

To plan the scaffolding you anticipate students will need during a project, use a "backward planning" process that starts with the major final product(s) students create in the project. The Student Learning Guide (created by the Buck Institute for Education and available at www.bie.org/object/document/project_design_overview_and_student_learning_guide) is a tool that can help you do this. See a completed example in the Appendix.

Here's the basic process:

1. List the major final products in the left column of the table. You may also include the "anchor standard" each product is meant to assess.

2. For each product, list the learning targets needed to complete it in the second column.

3. In the third column, list the formative assessment techniques or checkpoints that will help you and your students determine if they are on track.

4. In the fourth column, list the instructional strategies (e.g., lessons, activities, assignments, resources) that will be used to support all learners in reaching the learning goals.

Note: The Project Assessment Map, described on pages 116–117, can be used as the first step in creating the Student Learning Guide.

Differentiating with Content, Process, and Products

Upper elementary teacher Jim Bentley knows from experience that his students have a wide range of reading abilities, yet he wants every student to be able to discuss and think critically about the content they are studying. For a recent filmmaking project, students were reading nonfiction news stories about the science of climate change and the logistics of recycling organic waste. To make the content accessible for everyone, he used an online resource called Newsela (http://newsela.com) that publishes stories from the daily news at five different reading levels.

"I can have all my students read and talk about climate change or organic recycling. Using interactive features, I can annotate the text in advance [to scaffold understanding with clues and prompts] and have students respond. And it's all at the Lexile level that's appropriate for each of them," he says.

Bentley's example of differentiating content illustrates one of the key ways that teachers modify instruction in PBL to meet diverse learners' needs. Let's explore how you can differentiate instruction with content, process, and products.

Content

Students need to be able to access information in a variety of ways. Bentley differentiates content by providing access to information at different reading levels. In another PBL classroom, English teacher Kimberly Head-Trotter provides students with a choice of formats to access content, such as graphic novels, read-alouds, and audiobooks. Other teachers might curate a variety of resources on a shared project website or at learning stations.

John McCarthy, author of *So All Can Learn* (2017), offers this recommendation for differentiating content: "Use strategies like videos, discussions, readings, and visuals to give learners a variety of ways to connect. Learners will find that at least some of the displays of content make sense, which would not happen if only one mode of delivery is used" (p. 7).

Learning stations or centers will give students more choice about content. McCarthy elaborates, "One station might have a playlist of three videos from which students choose one to view. Another station gives details of how experts in the field use the skills or address the focused event. A third station includes several articles, while a fourth has the same articles on recordings for listening" (2017, p. 13).

Cheryl Bautista's 3rd grade class includes several students who are English language learners. Their individual language levels vary from beginner to nearly proficient in English. For each project, the teacher anticipates students' language needs and plans scaffolding accordingly.

The project about designing a tiny house, for example, involved math vocabulary she knew would be new to many of her English learners. Early in the project, Bautista introduced terms such as *perimeter* in small-group settings. "I would ask them, 'What do you think this word means?' Then we would draw pictures or use photographs to help them understand." Students made their own content-concept dictionaries in which each term was explained with a drawing, along with synonyms and antonyms. "This gave them their own reference to use throughout the project," Bautista explains.

Process

How do students make sense of what they are learning? That's likely to vary from one learner to the next, which is why it's also important to differentiate *process*. Tomlinson recommends providing students with options when it comes to how they process information and ideas. She elaborates with an example:

> A teacher can give students choices about how they express what they learn during a research exercise—providing options, for example, of creating a political cartoon, writing a letter to the editor, or making a diagram as a way of expressing what they understand about relations between the British and colonists at the onset of the American Revolution. (Tomlinson & Allen, 2000, p. 8)

Teacher Rebecca Newburn uses interactive science notebooks to document the inquiry process in PBL and scaffold instruction as needed with her middle school students. The structure of the notebooks builds in scaffolding (Macarelli, 2010).

As Newburn explains, "The right side [of the notebook] is teacher-provided information: readings, guided instruction, and so forth. The left side is student output. How do they interact with the content? How do they show their thinking?" One student might draw and label a diagram or concept map. Another might analyze data and produce a table or written summary.

"It's automatically differentiated," Newburn adds, with students choosing how they want to represent their thinking. She can follow up as needed with redirection or support for students who are struggling, or she can offer extension ideas for students who have mastered science concepts and are ready to go deeper with their inquiry.

Product

In PBL, students typically have choices when it comes to demonstrating their understanding at the end of a project. As McCarthy (2017) explains, "Effective products are aligned, authentic, and meaningful to learning outcomes. Giving students choices of products can increase the chances of students finding one that they believe they can do well" (p. 9).

The many project examples described in this book yielded a range of meaningful products, from documentary films to community action plans to family financial advice. Some teachers offer students a wide choice of how they will demonstrate what they know and can do. Others have all of their students produce the same product while still allowing room for differentiation. Every one of Bentley's students, for example, produced educational videos. All of Schneiderjohn's students wrote and enacted historical skits. But in each project, students had many choices to make when it came to their specific topic, script, set design, and editing.

Early elementary teacher Sara Lev makes it a point to involve students in determining their final products. "Usually, the kids have ideas about how they want to share their understandings," she says. "I know the key understandings I want us to get to, but I wait for the final product idea to come from students."

One year, for example, a literacy project about taking care of community spaces concluded with her transitional kindergarten students publishing an illustrated alphabet book ("*T* is for throwing away trash"). They donated their book to the school library to educate other students. When she introduced a similar project the next year, Lev recognized that her new class was ready for a more complex challenge to respond to this driving question: *How can we take care of the environment and inspire others to help us?*

"These students' depth of thinking was higher than I've experienced with other classes," Lev observes. "The word *responsibility* came up naturally in their conversations. They were thinking critically about how to solve problems." Eventually, student-and-teacher discussions led to the idea of students producing a training manual, how-to videos, and hands-on lessons demonstrating how to do specific jobs to take care of the school environment. They even generated ideas for innovative tools to make their jobs easier.

"These students were way beyond making an alphabet book," she says. "They would have finished that in a week." Instead, their more ambitious final product pushed them all to deeper learning while still allowing for individual differentiation. One child, whose learning challenges include speech, language, and attention issues, managed to invent "an incredible tool" (a brush to clean the tiny corners of a playhouse) and use the design thinking process to prototype and perfect her design. Other children with more advanced literacy skills were able to write informational texts and improve their presentation skills. "The project itself was differentiated enough," Lev says, for all students to experience growth.

Align Scaffolding with Learning Goals

Backward planning will help you align scaffolding to the learning goals of your project. When identifying learning goals, you considered what you want students to know and be able to do by the end of the project. You also brainstormed major products that would provide evidence of student learning, which aligned to standards. To plan for effective scaffolding, you need to unpack these products and determine what knowledge, understanding, and skills are necessary to complete them (Larmer et al., 2015). That information will help you create a Student Learning Guide that anticipates scaffolding needs.

Keeping in mind the specific needs of your students and the learning goals of your project, plan for a variety of instructional strategies to scaffold learning at key times during the project, especially when you anticipate challenges. Ray Ahmed knows that his chemistry students include many English language learners and a high percentage of students with special needs. He wants all students to be able to understand difficult scientific texts and conduct their own scientific research. Those academic skills are essential in the course. Students' final projects are treated as exit assessments that count toward graduation requirements.

"We read a lot of complex texts in this course," Ahmed acknowledges. Even though some readings are going to be challenging for many students, he doesn't want to "dumb down" the material for students who might struggle. Instead, he plans scaffolds to help all students access the texts and read for understanding.

Start with questions and predictions: Before handing out the thick text sets that students use throughout a project, Ahmed plans an entry event that prompts students to generate their own questions. This not only scaffolds inquiry but also serves as a prereading exercise. When he distributes texts, students see the readings as resources to help them answer their own questions. "This gives kids an opportunity in a low-stakes way to go through a set of readings and find answers to their own questions. They're reading for information."

Read together: "Some texts are hard. We read those together," Ahmed explains. Guiding the class through challenging texts creates opportunities for him to help students learn technical vocabulary and provide an introduction to unfamiliar scientific concepts. In the process, he's modeling literacy strategies that students can apply when they read on their own or discuss texts in small groups.

Support as needed: For students who need additional support with literacy skills, Ahmed and his coteacher (who has expertise in special education) provide additional support as needed. They might suggest that students use tools such as graphic organizers or note-catchers, or they might spend one-on-one conferencing time with students who need additional help.

Ahmed builds in additional support as projects near completion and students are preparing for presentations and scrutiny from public audiences. His English language learners might practice first in pairs and then trios, gradually working up to larger audiences. Ahmed will schedule after-school practice sessions for students who want more time. "One of the messages we talk about when we do anything hard is that we get smarter by putting in effort. The projects actually show that," he adds.

Anticipating when and why English learners may struggle with PBL is a good first step to planning appropriate scaffolds for them. For example, the process of doing PBL—which is different than traditional, teacher-directed learning—may pose linguistic or cultural barriers for students who have not had previous experience with student-centered learning. Mastery of content or acquisition of skills may prove challenging for different reasons. Acquisition of English language skills is another concern unique to this population. At different stages in a project, you can support English learners by introducing scaffolds to help them understand the project process, understand content, and make progress with language development. Figure 6.1 offers some suggestions.

PBL and Inclusion: Meeting All Needs

For students with special needs, PBL provides a vehicle for meaningful inclusion. Special education teacher Kristin Uliasz (2016), who is an inclusion and resource specialist in a PBL high school in Davis, California, points out that every project design element and all the Project Based Teaching Practices are geared toward creating "the kind of engaging and dynamic learning environment that is *also* known to best serve students with a wide range of disabilities" (2016, para. 6). Among her recommended strategies for success are the following:

Combine wisdom: When specialists and general educators team up on project planning and implementation, all students benefit. Uliasz, for example, is familiar with the specific needs of the students she works with individually and can advocate for instructional supports or accommodations they may need during a project. She relies on her classroom colleagues to be experts in their content areas. "Our combined wisdom makes it fairly easy to anticipate needs and embed considerations for the diverse range of students at the beginning stages of project design," she explains (2016, para. 9).

Differentiate instruction: One of the benefits of PBL, Uliasz argues, is that it is naturally differentiated. She elaborates, "By allowing students to take different paths and explore different interests in a project, this means that at any given time, students in the same class may be working on very different things. This normalizes the students who *need* different things, alleviates the stigma of support that students often bring with them into the classroom, and reinforces a

Figure 6.1 English Language Learner Scaffolds for PBL

The chart below provides scaffolding strategies and recommendations to support English language learners during each phase of the project process. The recommendations here align with the planned scaffolding strategies from the *Theoretical Foundations and Research Base for California's English Language Development Standards.*

	Scaffolding the Project Process	Scaffolding Content Learning	Scaffolding Language Development
	How can you reduce linguistic or cultural barriers to project completion and success?	*How can you reduce linguistic or cultural barriers to content or skill mastery?*	*How can you support students' acquisition of English language skills within the context of a project?*
Launching the Project: Entry Event + Driving Question	• Have students develop and use a BIE Project Team Work Plan to structure and organize their project work.[2,5] • Post due dates and tasks to be completed to a project wall (virtual or in the classroom).[2] • Use the Question Formulation Technique to help students understand how to create effective questions.[6] • Provide closed and open sentence frames to support question generation.[8] • Brainstorm and sort the questions generated by students. Sort questions into categories that are easy for students to identify (e.g., content questions, process questions, presentation questions).[8]	• Use a KWL chart[7], question frames, and explicit modeling[8] for the need to know list to help capture what students already know about the topic and to support students in asking new questions.[1,6] • During an entry event, use visual aids (e.g., photos, videos, physical objects) to help build context for learners at all levels of language proficiency.[7] • If the entry event is an "experience" (e.g., field trip, hands-on activity), have students use graphic organizers to keep their thoughts organized or to write key words that can serve as memory triggers. A scavenger hunt is a useful strategy for a field trip.[7] • Use a camera, if possible, for students to capture experiences during the entry event or to create visuals they can later use to recall information and develop connections.[7]	• Explicitly teach and define content-related vocabulary during the discussion of the entry event.[2] • Create and maintain a vocabulary wall for academic language associated with the project.[8] • Use entry events as an opportunity to introduce students to different types of texts and to discuss the conventions and purposes of text types.[4,8] • To provide more opportunities for low-stakes speaking and listening practice, have students discuss the entry event and need to knows in pairs or small groups before engaging in a whole-class discussion.[5] • Avoid (or explicitly teach) colloquialisms and idioms in project-related resources (e.g., entry events, driving questions, rubrics).[4]
Build Knowledge, Understanding, and Skills to Answer the Driving Question	• Post daily objectives in student-friendly language ("I can...") for content, skills, and language learning. Refer to these often. Note when objectives are differentiated for specific students.[2] • Use a variety of grouping strategies (e.g., heterogeneous, language level, pairs, self-selected) strategically throughout the course of a project.[5]	• Deliver instruction in a variety of formats (e.g., hands-on learning experiences, small-group lessons, direct instruction).[7] • Provide leveled texts for students during work time.[4] • Structure workshops in a logical sequence, providing clear modeling and explanations, as well as opportunities for guided practice.[2]	• Use observations and written tasks such as reflective journals to formatively assess student progress on language development targets.[3] • Have students develop personalized illustrated dictionaries to keep track of key vocabulary.[8] • Provide varied opportunities for speaking and listening (e.g., inner-outer circles, think-pair-share, jigsaw, role-plays).[5]

	• Have students work in linguistically diverse pairs or small groups to engage in reciprocal teaching or project content.[5] • Plan frequent opportunities for informal formative assessments (e.g., exit tickets, journals, whiparounds, conferences), and adjust instruction based on these assessments.[5]		• Provide sentence frames to help students give and receive feedback.[8] • When appropriate, provide students with exemplary writing samples and/or text frames to teach them about text and language conventions.[3]
Develop and Critique Products and Answers to the Driving Question	• Model and practice the use of structured protocols for critiquing work.[8] • Provide Thinking Maps to help students organize ideas and information.[7] • Co-create rubrics for final products and success skills with students. Both teachers and students should use the rubrics for assessment and reflection, and the same rubrics should be used for formative and summative assessment.[3]	• Use the Question Formulation Technique to guide students in developing new questions to refine their understanding of content.[6]	
Present Products and Answers to the Driving Question	• Have students work in groups to complete a BIE Presentation Plan.[7] • Provide multiple opportunities for students to practice their presentations and receive feedback.[2,3] • Record students as they practice presentations. Allow them to review the video and compare their performance to the presentation rubric, reflecting on opportunities for improvements.[3]	• Provide graphic organizers to help students organize their learning when observing one another's presentations.[7] • Encourage students to use visual aids and multimedia to enhance and clarify the content in their presentations.[7] • Have students use structured protocols to reflect on how this project builds on their existing knowledge and skills.[1]	• Work with students to identify the tone, level of formality, and linguistic style that are most appropriate for the presentation audience and context. Provide models to help students understand the appropriate "register."[8] • Provide language models for different aspects of presentations (e.g., giving instructions, describing processes, comparing and contrasting ideas).[8] • Provide question frames to support audience members in asking effective questions.[6]

[1] Taking into account what students already know, including primary language and culture, and relating it to what they are to learn.
[2] Selecting and sequencing tasks, such as modeling and explaining and providing guided practice in a logical order.
[3] Frequently checking for understanding during instruction, as well as gauging progress at appropriate intervals throughout the year.
[4] Choosing texts carefully for specific purposes (e.g., motivational, linguistic, content).
[5] Providing a variety of collaborative grouping processes.
[6] Constructing good questions that promote critical thinking and extended discourse.
[7] Using a range of information systems, such as graphic organizers, diagrams, photographs, videos, or other multimedia to enhance access to content.
[8] Providing students with language models, such as sentence frames/starters, academic vocabulary walls, language frame charts, exemplary writing samples, or teaching language modeling (e.g., using academic vocabulary or phrasing).

culture of individuality and self-management that leads to students' owning their learning" (2016, para. 11).

Embed IEP goals into projects: Embed students' specific academic IEP goals throughout their differentiated project pathways. This allows you to address those skills with consistency. In a PBL classroom, the emphasis on key success skills provides daily opportunities to work on these goals in an authentic and natural context.

When PBL takes places in an inclusive classroom where all students' needs are addressed, students don't get labeled. Chemistry teacher Ray Ahmed and his coteacher are careful not to treat students as "mine" or "yours." Rather than having his colleague work only with students with special needs, Ahmed prefers a model where "all our kids are our responsibilities." His coteacher brings a knowledge of tools and strategies that help students with special needs—and all students. "My job," Ahmed adds, "is to create a culture where all the gifts of our students are brought out."

Here are some more examples of scaffolding to prime your thinking (Alber, 2014; Tomlinson, quoted in Rebora, 2008):

- **Model learning strategies** using fishbowls and think-alouds and by sharing samples of student work.
- **Tap prior knowledge** and connect to students' cultural understandings by having them share hunches, generate need-to-know questions, or make know-wonder-learn (KWL) charts.
- **Structure discussions** using protocols such as think-pair-share, see-think-wonder, and Socratic seminars. Introduce sentence stems to use during academic conversations and post them in a visible place so all students can access them as needed to participate in discussions. (For example, model how to disagree with sentence stems that begin, "Here's another way to think about that..." or "I see your point, but have you considered...?")
- **Team up** bilingual students with English language learners, as circumstances allow. Bilingual students can help their peers with pronunciation, content, and confidence building.

- **Preteach key vocabulary** using photos, analogies, met-aphors, or drawings. This strategy is especially helpful for English language learners, who can then build on their knowl-edge of academic vocabulary as the project proceeds.
- **Introduce visual aids** such as graphic organizers or word walls. Math and science teachers often use mini-whiteboards on which students show their problem solving.
- **Leverage technology** such as HyperDocs for digital les-sons, interactive journals to scaffold the inquiry process, and screencasts for just-in-time learning.
- **Offer workshops and mini-lessons** to support students who need to build key skills and understanding for project suc-cess. Students can self-select workshops or be invited based on your formative assessment results.

For most teachers, scaffolding in PBL includes a blend of tools and strategies. When Sara Lev plans learning activities for a project, she includes scaffolds to set her transitional kindergarten students up for success. Graphic organizers are helpful for students who are English language learners and those who are more visual learners, for example. Along with physical scaffolds, she also uses students' questions and comments to support their classmates' thinking.

"If I have three or four kids who participate in discussions right away, I can use their comments as scaffolding. I might repeat some-thing one of them says and say, 'This reminds me of…' or I might say, 'Look, Alec has this cool idea to make a tool' or 'Molly has this ques-tion.' That's different than if I showed them what I want them to do. The modeling is not coming from an adult—it's from their peer. I think that's a hook for them. It says, 'I can do it, too.'"

Just-in-Time Scaffolds

During the same project, some students may get stuck, whereas oth-ers may need to stretch. Just-in-time scaffolds help you tailor the sup-port or challenge to meet students' immediate needs.

Students in Telannia Norfar's precalculus class, for example, were well into a project that challenged them to provide financial planning advice to actual clients from the community. Their clients' needs were diverse. Some families wanted advice about saving for their children's college education. Others were focused on saving for retirement or buying a house. Some had multiple financial goals.

At project launch, Norfar introduced students to their clients using photos and stories. Engagement appeared to be high as students realized these were real people—not assignments from a math book. Students were excited to learn they would have opportunities to meet with their clients face to face. Many students also made connections to their own financial situations, which heightened engagement.

"Most of my students will be the first in their families to go to college," the teacher explains. "That means they are literally on their own to figure out how to make that happen. There's no one at home who knows how it all works, including the financial part. So even though we're helping another family, I am helping my students understand college planning. They have personal connections to the project."

That initial excitement started to wane, however, when it was time for mathematical problem solving. Students suddenly had to apply their understanding of exponential, logarithmic, and rational functions to design financial plans tailored to clients' goals and current financial situations. "If you don't understand the principles of these functions," Norfar cautioned students, "you can get burned."

In a whole-class lesson, she introduced students to a general formula for making financial calculations. Their next assignment was to manipulate that formula so it would apply to their clients' specific situations. Norfar was surprised by the frustration that surfaced in their need-to-know discussion. "Many students wanted to know, 'How can we do this easily?' I thought, 'Darn it!'" the teacher recalls with a laugh. "I didn't intend to scaffold everything for them."

Based on her formative assessment, Norfar recognized that some students understood the math concepts well enough to derive formulas on their own; they just needed encouragement to keep going. A pep talk about persistence—and a reminder that their clients were depending on them for answers—was all the scaffolding they needed.

Others were struggling with the math. They needed the just-in-time support Norfar was able to provide via mini-lessons, workshops, and modeling of sample formulas. "They needed that content help," she realized, before they were ready to resume working on their clients' financial plans.

Let's consider two more learning goals that may call for additional scaffolding during projects: success skills (including self-management) and disciplinary thinking.

Scaffolding Success Skills

When you identified learning goals for your project during the design and plan stage, you focused on specific success skills along with content mastery. Helping students become better at collaboration, critical thinking, communication, and creativity are common project goals. Coupled with academic mastery, these "four Cs" provide essential preparation for college, careers, and citizenship. Similarly, the self-management skills of setting goals, maintaining focus, and managing time effectively support students' success in PBL—and in life.

Don't assume that students will develop these success skills automatically or all at the same pace. Instead, provide scaffolding as needed—and informed by formative assessment—to help students become more capable and confident with the targeted success skills.

As the project unfolds, continue to provide necessary scaffolding for the success skills you are seeking to develop. If the learning goal is collaboration, for example, how will you scaffold teamwork? If it's critical thinking, how will you help students develop arguments based on reliable evidence or understand cause-and-effect relationships? Consider students' prior experiences with the targeted success skills, stay alert for any struggles, and plan scaffolding accordingly.

Use protocols and routines to focus on specific aspects of success skills that are challenging for students. For example, reaching consensus among team members is an important aspect of collaboration. Students need to understand that consensus is not the same as "majority rules" or "loudest voice wins." Instead, it requires listening to diverse perspectives and arriving at a decision that the entire team supports.

As we heard earlier, social studies teacher Erin Brandvold used a protocol called GOILS—Groups of Increasingly Larger Size—to help her students reach consensus about a scoring guide for their revolutions project. Another protocol that takes the mystery out of consensus building is called "Fist to Five" (Boss, 2013; Fletcher, 2002; Rindone, 1996). Students use the following hand signals to communicate their positions on a decision or proposed solution:

- Fist (no fingers): "No way. I need to talk more about this and see changes before I can support it."
- 1 finger: "Learning toward no. I still want to discuss and suggest changes."
- 2 fingers: "So-so. I am more comfortable with the proposal but would like to discuss some minor tweaks."
- 3 fingers: "It's OK. I'm not in total agreement but can support this without further discussion."
- 4 fingers: "Yes. I think it's a good idea/decision."
- 5 fingers: "Absolutely! This is a great idea, and I will help lead its implementation."

Team members who hold up three or fewer fingers are given time to air their concerns. Discussions continue until all team members can signal consensus for an idea by showing three or more fingers.

If the targeted success skill is critical thinking, scaffold students' argumentation skills by introducing sentence starters:

- "I understand your point, but here's another way to think about that..."
- "Have you considered...?"
- "I disagree because..."

If the targeted success skill is creativity, scaffold idea generation by modeling strategies for effective brainstorming, teaching students how to use simple sketches or storyboards to make their ideas visible and discussable, or warming up creative thinking with a game or puzzle. When Jim Bentley's student filmmakers were generating initial ideas for their educational videos, they needed to think creatively about recycling. Bentley explains their underlying challenge: "How could we persuade a business to do something that might potentially be perceived as a burden? We had to come up with creative examples that would inspire business owners."

To scaffold creativity, Bentley had students work first in small teams to generate as many ideas as they could. He encouraged divergent thinking, advising students to generate ideas without pausing to edit or censor their creativity. Once the teams finished brainstorming, they came back together as a whole class to discuss and debate ideas. "Through that process, we reached consensus about seven stories we wanted to pursue," the teacher says. "Each team took ownership for one story."

Sara Lev taught her students the design thinking process to scaffold their problem-solving skills. They were midway through a project about taking care of the environment when one boy suggested inventing a tool to assist in doing a specific job. His idea sparked other students' creativity. "Then we used the design thinking process to draw our ideas, make prototypes, and present our ideas to each other," Lev explains. Design strategies such as SCAMPER (Substitute, Combine, Adapt, Modify, Put to another use, Eliminate, Reverse) are useful scaffolds for helping students come up with creative solutions.

Scaffold students' communication skills by modeling and using fishbowls and role-plays to help them understand the benefits of effective speaking and listening skills. For example, if students are preparing to talk with experts, spend time as a whole class on good interview questions and follow-ups, and have students practice interviewing their peers before meeting the experts.

Near the end of a project, you may notice that students are nervous about sharing their results with a public audience. To scaffold their communication skills, build in ample time for low-risk practice sessions before the actual event. You might start by having each team present to another team or record themselves on video and do a self-critique. Then, after more fine-tuning and practice, teams could present to the whole class or to another class. With each presentation, make sure the audiences know how to offer constructive feedback, and make sure students have time to apply feedback to improve their presentations.

To build students' self-management skills, help them use calendars, project trackers, and other project management tools (discussed in Chapter 4) to become more independent learners who can manage their own workflow in a project. As always, be ready to support students when they run into challenges or setbacks.

Partway through a math project, Telannia Norfar noticed that many students were struggling to work semi-independently. "When they tried to work on their own with their teammates, they were not so successful. They told me they didn't want so much freedom. We regrouped," she says, "and I took back the reins for a while."

One helpful scaffold was a team planning guide. It outlined specific roles and responsibilities for students within each team—such as communications director, mathematician lead, and project manager. "I gave them a form to fill out each day about which tasks each person was doing on the project. They needed that template," Norfar realized, to learn to be accountable to themselves and to one another.

Meanwhile, two of her more motivated and self-directed students were ready to charge ahead. They didn't need daily task reminders. Norfar encouraged them to move at a more accelerated pace, using their need-to-know questions to prompt additional research. "They were able to keep progressing by returning to their own questions," she observed.

PBL veterans help students find learning opportunities even in the face of failure. Chemistry teacher Ray Ahmed, for example, gives his 11th graders considerable freedom during their second semester to design their own projects based on questions that interest them. "Some kids are so excited by their idea that I let them go with it, even if I haven't figured out how to help them make that idea better. If they fail along the way, they realize that it wasn't such a good idea. Should they stop and change directions? Are there parts of this project that we can tweak and make better? What are the pieces we can build on? We talk about that. I remind them that this is what adults do [in scientific research]. They have to grapple with dilemmas about their research. Now we have a chance to learn together. Thinking through those things with students is so valuable," he says, and it reinforces a culture of learning that tolerates risk taking.

Frequent check-ins with students enable Ahmed to identify trouble early enough so there's time to regroup. Helping students recover from failure is part of scaffolding, too. Through his one-on-one discussions, Ahmed helps students develop the mental muscle to persist through challenges. When students tap into their capacity to take risks and overcome failures, they're learning more than chemistry. "When students realize, 'I have control over my project,' they're learning, 'I have control over my life and the decisions I make,'" Ahmed says.

As students gain confidence with success skills, encourage them to reflect on their growth as more independent, self-directed learners.

◯ Try This: Teach Presentation Skills

Not all projects involve a presentation to an audience—there are other ways to make students' work public—but many do, and it's easy to overlook the need to teach presentation skills. As a project progresses, most of the teacher's and students' energy is focused on completing products and arriving at an answer to the driving question. But when it's time for students to share their work with an audience, poor presentations can seriously detract from the experience.

To build students' presentation skills, keep the following ideas in mind:

- Consider teaching speaking skills and the use of presentation media early in the school year *before* doing a project. This will also save time during the project.

- Help students understand what good speaking skills are by cocreating or providing a rubric (such as those found at www.bie.org/objects/cat/rubrics) or another set of criteria and then using it to critique examples of presentations (e.g., TED Talks).

> **⊙ Try This: Teach Presentation Skills (*continued*)**
>
> - Provide lessons, resources, and guided practice to improve specific speaking skills, such as using emotion, storytelling, avoiding common verbal errors, and making eye contact.
>
> - Steer students to examples and resources that help improve their visual design skills for creating effective posters, displays, and multimedia graphics.
>
> - Make sure students understand how to adapt their speech and tailor a presentation to a particular context, task, and audience.
>
> - Have students practice their presentations several times. Teams can present to one another or to a test audience for formative feedback. Alternatively, they can record themselves on video to self-critique.
>
> - Provide students with a form or template for planning their presentation, such as the example in Figure 6.2, which is for elementary or middle school students.

Scaffolding Disciplinary Thinking

PBL often puts students into authentic roles. They may be challenged to act as scientists, mathematicians, historians, architects, engineers, documentarians, or authors to solve problems or create original products. This requires learning to think in a way that experts do within their respective disciplines.

For middle school teacher and PBL veteran Tom Neville, a key learning goal is to develop strong historical thinking in all his students. In some projects, students have focused on a highly local problem, such as investigating and documenting the history of a single alley in Washington, DC (www.lifeinthealley.org). Other projects are more global in scope. The Monuments Project involves students from different countries collaborating to tell the stories of American World War I veterans buried abroad.

Figure 6.2 Presentation Planner for Students

PRESENTATION PLAN

What my presentation is about: _____

_____

Who is my audience? _____

_____

What do I want my audience to know, feel, or do? _____

_____

How will I begin my presentation? _____

_____

What will be in the middle part of my presentation? _____

_____

How will I end my presentation? _____

_____

What will I show or do to make my presentation interesting? _____

_____

To help students think and research as historians, Neville introduces a variety of tools and protocols from his teacher toolbox. Many of these would be useful for any history classroom; however, he uses them strategically in PBL to help students meet learning goals while reinforcing a culture of inquiry. For example, Neville appreciates the Critical Exploration approach developed by Eleanor Duckworth (www.criticalexplorers.org) because he says it teaches his students "to patiently observe, to ground observations in specific evidence others can see, to listen to others' observations, to identify patterns between observations, to be comfortable sharing uncertainty and simply being in a state of uncertainty, and to embrace the idea that there always might be more you didn't notice or know."

Neville also uses the Question Formulation Technique developed by the Right Question Institute (http://rightquestion.org/education)

to scaffold student inquiry. He uses critique protocols for peer feedback and other protocols as needed to build disciplinary thinking. "All of these provide a framework for thinking about evidence and reference points for check-ins throughout the year," he says.

Getting comfortable with a new protocol "can feel slow at first," he admits, but it's time well spent. Over time, students come to see protocols as tools for thinking. "These [protocols] acclimate students to slower thinking; encourage careful, refined questioning; build openness to wide ranges of evidence and perspective; yield an ability to give and get honest feedback; and push students to constantly reflect and reiterate."

Similarly, chemistry teacher Ray Ahmed wants his students to think and investigate in the same way that professional scientists do. One aspect of scientific thinking is asking questions that can be tested with experiments. "This is hard," the teacher acknowledges, especially when students are new to doing chemistry investigations. When students are building background knowledge by reading journal articles and other source material, Ahmed uses protocols to encourage question asking, such as, "What do I want to know? What do I need to know?" (See Figure 7.1 on page 167.) Once students generate a list of their questions, they categorize them into questions that are easily answerable versus questions that require investigation, questions that are closed versus questions that are open-ended. "We found through our first pass that students didn't have questions that would lead to a scientific investigation. They were learning a lot of information, but we didn't have an experiment."

To scaffold inquiry in the first project of the year, Ahmed introduces an authentic problem that is rich with good questions to investigate in the chemistry lab. A recent example was discovering the causes of the water crisis in Flint, Michigan. "It was sort of a forced choice," he acknowledges, "in that it pushed kids into this idea of what a corrosive inhibitor is and what's the best one." Once he introduced the topic, students were off and running with their own questions. "After that [first] question, everything else was theirs—the materials they picked, how they planned the experiment, the type of data they wanted to collect, and how they wanted to analyze their data."

Many of Ahmed's students are English language learners. The quality of their final project work, which is critiqued by experts and shared with authentic audiences, "highlights that these kids can engage in really higher-order thinking in a way that honors who they are as individuals."

Rebecca Alber (2014), an *Edutopia* blogger and instructor at UCLA's Graduate School of Education, reminds teachers of the wisdom of taking time to support learners, even if that means slowing down. "I often say to teachers that they have to slow down in order to go quickly. Scaffolding a lesson may, in fact, take longer to teach, but the end product is of far greater quality and the experience much more rewarding for all involved" (para. 19).

Coaches' Notebook: Scaffold Teacher Learning

Just as students benefit from differentiated instruction to help them succeed at projects, teachers' needs for PBL support also vary widely. To scaffold teacher learning when it comes to PBL practices, instructional coach Andrew Miller (2017) offers his colleagues a menu of offerings for personalized professional development:

> Just as we model voice and choice with students, we should do the same with our teachers. They deserve voice and choice in how they learn to better implement PBL. After all, all teachers are in different places in their professional growth. Perhaps teachers need a planning session for a project. Or they might need to unpack standards to ensure alignment. Teachers also value observing each other implement specific milestones of a PBL project. I experimented with a PBL Coaching Menu and found that teachers enjoyed not only the choice itself but that the choices had differing levels of commitment. By offering voice and choice, you can create a variety of entry points into coaching. (para. 6)

What belongs on a PBL Coaching Menu? Miller's version (see Figure 6.3) includes "Appetizers," such as generating project ideas

Figure 6.3   PBL Coaching Menu

Instructional
Coaching Menu

We want to provide you with professional learning that meets your needs regardless of your experience. You can select items from this menu in any order, at anytime.

Appetizer

Project Ideation

Visit with your coach at a time that is right for you to brainstorm ideas for projects, products and driving questions. A short amount of time leads to great project ideas!

Observe a Colleague

Do you know a colleague that does PBL well? A coach will cover your class so that you can walk a teacher implementing a project. You will also debrief the visit with the coach and colleague.

Unpack Standards and Targets

Want to examine and figure out the right standards and outcomes to target in a project? Collaborate with your peers to unpack standards and identify standards that you might teach and assess in a future project.

Main Course

Coaching Cycle

Do you have a general concern about teaching and learning in your classroom? Is there something related or unrelated to PBL you want to improve upon. This options starts with a session to identify a challenge or problem of practice, observation, and then reflective debrief.

Co-Teaching

Work with a coach to co-teach a component of your PBL project. Struggle to form teams? Need help launching a project? Want to support students to effectively critique of their products? Here you can focus on one element of PBL project implementation with a collaborative partner.

PBL Project Implementation

Collaborate with a cohort of colleagues to plan and implement a full project. You will create your own essential questions to drive your professional learning, meet regularly with your cohort, visit each other's classroom, and engage in a cycle of reflective practice with your coach over the course of 5-6 weeks.

Looking at Student Work

Bring an assessment/ task and related student work from your project (formative or summative) to engage in a protocol with a small team of colleagues to improve the project and assessment of student learning.

Dessert

Coaches Cafe/ Cocktail Hour

Coaches will offer informal "office hours" over coffee and cocktails. Visit as long as you want, talk to colleagues, and pick up something to read.

Plan an Exhibition

Work with the coach and other colleagues to plan an exhibition of your project(s) to allow for community and parent feedback, and to celebrate what students have accomplished.

Technology Support

Get just in time support to learn a technology tool during your planning time.

Project Reflection and Goal Setting

After you implement a project, the learning isn't over. Work with your coach to document your learning and reflection, and set goals to improve your teaching and/or project for next time.

Source: Used with permission from Andrew Miller, Shanghai American School.

or observing a colleague during project implementation; a "Main Course," such as coteaching part of a project or looking at student work with colleagues; and "Dessert" activities, such as planning a project exhibition or reflecting at the close of a project.

Strategies to Scaffold Student Learning: Key Takeaways

Take time to reflect on the many scaffolding strategies you have read about in this chapter.

- During projects, how might you make more deliberate use of the scaffolding tools and strategies that are familiar to you and your students (such as graphic organizers, quizzes, or leveled readers)?
- As you plan for scaffolding in PBL, are you considering the needs of all learners? Which supports will everyone need to be successful? Which scaffolds will certain students or groups of students need most?
- How might you improve learning outcomes in PBL by differentiating with content, process, and products?
- Have you planned for scaffolding to support students' success skills, such as self-management?
- How will you help students learn to think as experts do? How will you scaffold disciplinary thinking?

On Your PBL Bookshelf

Academic Conversations: Classroom Talk That Fosters Critical Thinking and Content Understandings: Jeff Zwiers and Marie Crawford introduce practical communication strategies to generate more productive, academically rich, and respectful classroom discussions that engage all students.

Causes and Cures in the Classroom: Getting to the Root of Academic and Behavior Problems: Margaret Searle addresses both academic and behavioral challenges that can interfere with learning, offering strate-gies for diagnosis and targeted interventions to get students back on track.

Developing Natural Curiosity Through Project-Based Learning: Five Strategies for the PreK–3 Classroom: Dayna Laur and Jill Ackers bring authentic PBL to life in the primary years with plentiful examples and strategies that address the needs of young learners, including literacy and language acquisition.

Differentiation in Middle and High School and *Differentiation in the Elementary Grades*: With their two books focusing on different grade levels, Kristina Doubet and Jessica Hockett offer upgraded differentia-tion strategies and tools designed to better meet the needs of today's diverse learners.

How to Differentiate Instruction in Academically Diverse Class-rooms (3rd ed.): Differentiated instruction authority Carol Ann Tom-linson combines theory and practice in this updated third edition. Although not specific to PBL, her insights on lesson design will help teachers differentiate projects by matching content, process, and products to learner readiness and interests.

Make Just One Change: Teach Students to Ask Their Own Ques-tions: To scaffold inquiry and inspire more student-centered learning, Dan Rothstein and Luz Santana recommend their Question Formula-tion Technique. This widely adopted protocol elevates student voice and encourages students to ask better questions to drive their own learning.

So All Can Learn: A Practical Guide to Differentiation: John McCar-thy uses plentiful classroom examples to show how differentiation can make a difference for all learners.

Teaching Gifted Kids in Today's Classroom: Susan Winebren-ner and contributing author Dina Brulles deliver helpful advice and resources for engaging and challenging gifted students in mixed-ability classrooms.

Well Spoken: Teaching Speaking to All Students: Erik Palmer offers strategies to help students improve their presentation and communi-cation skills.

7

Engage and Coach

*Engaging and coaching strategies build intrinsic motivation
and help students achieve their own learning goals.*

Sara Lev was on a field trip to an architecture and design firm with
her transitional kindergarten students when she had a flash of insight
about what it means to engage and coach students. By this point, they
were well into a project about designing an outdoor playhouse for
their school. Students had previously created floor plans of their proposed playhouse designs. The field trip would give them the chance
to learn about the design process from experts, see how architects
use models, and work on building their own 3D models. The goal for
the day was for each child to leave the studio with a cardboard model
based on his or her floor plan.

As Lev scanned the studio full of busy 5-year-olds, she noticed
one student in particular. In class, Zoe was usually outgoing and
quick to participate. She shared her ideas and extended her learning.
So Lev was surprised to see her sitting alone with her floor plan and
materials, not even starting to build a model.

Taking a seat beside her, the teacher asked, "What's going on,
Zoe?"

No answer.

The teacher waited. Finally, Zoe said, "This is too hard."

"What is too hard?"

"Making this." Zoe pointed to her floor plan.

Lev reflected for a moment on what she heard the child say, then responded, "Oh, trying to make your plan feels really hard? What feels hard about it?"

"I can't make this." Zoe pointed to her detailed drawing that included labels for "a kite," "a basement," and other design elements that had sprung from her imagination.

Without another word, Lev took a piece of cardboard and started moving it around, folding it in different ways, making shapes. Then she said, "Well, a lot of models here start with a base. Like a bottom part. Do you want to try that?"

No reply.

"Is there one part of your floor plan you want to start with?"

Zoe didn't answer. She just kept staring at her plan, as if to say, "I can't make this out of cardboard. It won't look right."

Then Lev looked at all the parts of her plan and noticed a label that read, "playhouse on wheels."

"Wait, Zoe, your house is on wheels. This is so cool! I haven't seen anyone's design have that. Do you want to start with that?"

A tiny, tiny smile crossed her face.

"How could we make a wheel?" the teacher asked, starting to shape the cardboard into a cylinder. Zoe took the cardboard out of her teacher's hands, got some duct tape, and wrapped it around the cylinder.

"That looks *just* like a wheel!" Lev told her.

Zoe started bending another piece of thin board into a diamond shape. "Hey, this can be the basement," the child said while she worked. "This is the same shape as my basement." And she taped it down.

Zoe was off and running. Lev left her to her work, checking back every five minutes or so. Finally, Zoe brought her completed model to show off.

"Zoe, did you notice what happened today?" Lev asked after admiring the model. "When you first sat down, you didn't think you could do it."

"I thought it was too hard," Zoe said, "but it wasn't."

Lev realized that she was witnessing a child's transformation from self-doubt to self-pride. And to observe a young child self-aware enough to *notice* her own transformation? That was downright inspiring.

Later, as she thought about what had transpired that day in the architecture studio, Lev asked herself, "What were my teacher moves? I observed. I listened. I reflected back what I heard her say and feel. I scaffolded without direct instruction by casually demonstrating what she *might* try, but I waited for her to take it in, to integrate it. I noticed a very special and original part of her idea and drew it out, calling it to her attention. I trusted her to work on her own when she seemed like she could, gradually releasing the responsibility from me to her. I returned to her periodically to check in. And in the end, I helped her see what she had learned."

This brief encounter—just a few moments during a much longer PBL experience—shows why engaging and coaching students is such an important aspect of Project Based Teaching. Strategies for engaging and coaching help you bring out the best in your students. Engagement often starts with building on students' interests and strengths, as we saw Lev do when she pointed out the originality of Zoe's design. Some projects open students' eyes to new interests, engaging them in challenges and topics they didn't even know they cared about. Once students are engaged, coaching strategies employ questioning, modeling, and reflection to help students persist through challenges to meet their goals.

If you've watched a seasoned PBL teacher in action, you may think that coaching and engagement are second nature. Dig a little deeper and you often find that PBL teachers also wear the coaching hat in athletics, debate, drama, or another extracurricular activity. As with every other aspect of PBL, there's more to the story than having a knack for relating to students. Engaging and coaching are learnable skills that get better with practice.

For those new to the teacher-as-coach role, it helps to break down this practice into its component parts. Let's take a closer look at how we engage and coach in PBL. In many ways, this practice overlaps with building a positive classroom culture (as discussed in Chapter 1) and depends on fostering a caring, trusting relationship between teacher and students.

★ Gold Standard Project Based Teaching Strategies: Engage and Coach

Strategies to engage and coach students are important throughout PBL. Indicators for Engage and Coach from the Project Based Teaching Rubric include the following points:

- The teacher's knowledge of individual student strengths, interests, backgrounds, and lives is used to engage them in the project and inform instructional decision making.

- Students and teacher use standards to codefine goals and benchmarks for the project in developmentally appropriate ways (e.g., by constructing a rubric together).

- Students' enthusiasm for and sense of ownership of the project is maintained by the shared nature of the work between teachers and students.

- Student questions play the central role in driving the inquiry and product development process; the driving question is actively used to sustain inquiry.

- Appropriately high expectations for the performance of all students are clearly established, shared, and reinforced by teachers and students.

- Individual student needs are identified through close relationships built with the teacher; needs are met not only by the teacher but by students themselves or other students, acting independently.

- Students and teacher reflect regularly and formally throughout the project on what (content) and how (process) students are learning; they specifically note and celebrate gains and accomplishments.

See the Appendix for the complete Project Based Teaching Rubric.

A Closer Look at Coaching and Engagement

During his long and storied career, tennis great Andre Agassi worked with all kinds of coaches. Some pushed his physical limits. Others challenged him emotionally. One helped him think like a chess player, plotting strategies to use against different opponents. His best coaches played to his strengths, worked with him to overcome weaknesses, and helped him reach the demanding goals he set for himself. "Coaching is not what you know," he told the *Harvard Business Review*. "It's what your student learns. And for your student to learn, you have to learn him" (quoted in Beard, 2015, para. 15).

Coaching extends far beyond athletics, of course. For virtually every endeavor, from running a business to getting fit to planning for retirement, there's a business/fitness/life coach available to help you improve your performance.

Education is no exception. The late Ted Sizer (2004), progressive educator and founder of the Coalition of Essential Schools, coined the term *teacher as coach* to describe the emerging role of the classroom teacher. As the goals of education expand beyond content mastery, it's no longer enough for teachers to be knowledge dispensers. To help students become more self-directed learners who can navigate a complex world, teachers need an expanded repertoire of strategies, including engaging and coaching.

In academics, as in athletics, a capable coach is an expert in content, knows how to develop students' individual skills, provides motivation, and builds effective teams. Education expert Carol Ann

Tomlinson (2011) adds more detail to the teacher-as-coach metaphor: "The best coaches encourage young people to work hard, keep going when it would be easier to stop, risk making potentially painful errors, try again when they stumble, and learn to love the sport. Not a bad analogy for a dynamic classroom" (para. 3).

Becoming a skillful classroom coach doesn't mean you stop teaching. Far from it. Jean Kugler, a PBL veteran from Columbus, Ohio, describes coaching as an evolution in your teaching style. "It's about maximizing student learning from start to finish, helping students stay motivated to reach high expectations. As a coach, you are building students' confidence and competence," she says.

Your teaching moves will naturally evolve as you get accustomed to the teacher-as-coach role. As you gain experience with PBL, Kugler adds, "you don't need to put so much emphasis on checking and monitoring." Those practices become part of your routine. "You're coaching students toward a higher level of performance."

Admittedly, learning to be a classroom coach may require unlearning, updating, or replacing some traditional teaching habits, such as being the expert. When former teacher and author Kirsten Olson (2014) went through a training program to be certified as a coach, she had to give up "the knowledge-bearing mantle of the teacher." It's not that your wisdom and content knowledge is no longer important. Rather, coaching challenges you to "become the inquirer, the question asker, the curiosity fomenter. When you coach, you…start getting really curious about what is going on with the other person (or people)" (para. 6).

When teachers develop what Olson (2014) describes as a "coaching stance," their classrooms become learning environments that foster creativity, encourage student voice and choice, and promote equity by rebalancing the traditional student-teacher power relationship.

For chemistry teacher Ray Ahmed, the frequent use of conferences has helped him get to know his students better so he can engage and coach them throughout projects. "We meet all the time," he explains, with each student signing up on a class calendar for at least one individual conference each week. The teacher does not set the agenda. Instead, students choose what they want to discuss. To help them envision what this looks like, Ahmed and his coteacher role-play a conference session.

The first conferences of the year are opportunities for teacher and students to get to know each other. Students might share their interests, ask questions about the rubric they use throughout the course, or ask for help understanding a concept they have discussed as a whole class. "It's low stakes," the teacher emphasizes, "and students realize we can talk about what they need. Some kids are scared of feedback at first. In conferences, they get to take the lead. And I can play the long game. I might start with a simple 'Good job' if that's what they need to hear right then."

As the weeks go by and the learning goals become more challenging, conferences get more serious in both tone and content. "Kids are self-assessing. They know what they're struggling with," Ahmed says, "and so do I." Conferences allow him and his coteacher to spend more individual time with students who need the most support.

Since introducing conferences to his teaching strategies, Ahmed says his conversations with students have improved. "Before this, most of our contacts were very transactional. We were checking this, checking that. It was never an ongoing conversation about the work that students were doing." By adding conferences to his coaching practices, the whole learning experience "feels more authentic to the students. They feel like they're part of the conversation and not just being talked to."

Coaching and engaging are important throughout projects, but certain teacher moves are worth emphasizing at key moments. Let's look closer at opportunities to engage and coach at the beginning, middle, and end of a project.

Engage at Project Launch

If you have considered students' interests, concerns, and background in the design of the project, students are more likely to be engaged from the get-go. Indeed, some projects get off to a good start because the inspiration came from students themselves. In other situations, however, the project (and teacher's passion) inspires students to engage with an issue they didn't even know they cared about.

Regardless of the inspiration for the project, you want to engage all learners from the outset, or it can feel like a long, uphill slog to the finish line. Project launch is an opportunity to provoke students' curiosity and connect them to the project on an emotional level. When students are invested in a project, they understand why it's worth doing—even if the work ahead appears challenging. From the start, you convey high expectations for what students will be able to achieve.

Ray Ahmed launched into a project with his chemistry students on their first day of class. When students arrived, they were greeted with an assortment of images and news stories set up around the room for a gallery walk. Some were accounts of a water crisis in Flint, Michigan, which has disproportionately affected people of color and low-income families. Others showed mold in the New York City housing projects where many students live. Still more evidence described the contamination of Gowanus Canal, a Superfund site that empties into New York Harbor. Ahmed challenged students to investigate these artifacts as if they were solving a mystery, asking, "What do you think is happening? What questions do you have?" The See/Think/Wonder protocol helped focus student observations and elicit questions.

That provocation was enough to get students talking about the bigger issues Ahmed wanted to uncover with them in the coming weeks. He explained, "The underlying idea of this project is environment racism. What is it? Does it exist in our community? What can we do about it?" Knowing that students were embarking on a complex project that would last several weeks, Ahmed also wanted them to make an emotional connection to the topic.

Ahmed sees the water crisis of Flint, Michigan, as a compelling case study that helps students not only learn about chemistry topics such as corrosion and contamination but also consider issues of social justice. "It puts a lens on something that has gone so terribly wrong," he said. By connecting the Flint crisis to similar issues in students' own backyards, "we get kids to start thinking about the world outside of where they live. By 11th grade, they're ready for that." The entry event set the stage for Ahmed's students to take on the role of scientist and answer the driving questions: *As chemists, what can we do about situations like Flint? What is the best corrosive inhibitor?*

The engagement that the gallery walk and discussions generated on the first day carried over to subsequent days as students got more immersed in hard science. Ahmed explained, "From talking about what we think is happening [in the examples], we start thinking about what we want to do." Students readily made the connection between their own questions and the subsequent chemistry labs and research. "We launch in so kids have questions and make predictions. We start doing research, which means more questions. And once they have questions that become testable, we can design and run experiments," Ahmed said, summarizing his approach to doing PBL in the sciences.

Cheryl Bautista was about to start an elections project with her 3rd graders. Although her students were still a decade away from voting age, she wanted to help them see themselves as future voters. She and her grade-level colleagues designed the project to address important content in social studies, including the role of elections and the rights of citizens in a democracy. They timed the project to coincide with national elections in the fall, when student interest in the democratic process was high.

Teachers started building anticipation a week before the project formally launched. They set out a ballot box in the classroom without saying a word to students about its purpose. "When it was time for PE on the first day, we looked in the empty ballot box and said, 'Oh, I guess no one voted. So, we'll just tell you what to do for PE today.'" The next day, students were quick to fill out ballots and choose which games they would play during PE.

But on the third day, teachers switched it up again. "We said, 'Sorry, only girls can vote today!'" Bautista recalls. That provoked plenty of discussion, especially among the boys. "Another day, we put ballot boxes in all the 3rd grade classrooms—but then we 'closed' one early, so students had to go find another polling place."

By the time the project formally launched, "everyone had something to remember about voting. They all had feelings about elections" and some new vocabulary (such as *polling places*). "They were getting the idea, from personal experience, that voting does make a difference," Bautista said.

Making that personal, emotional connection to an issue or challenge is the goal of an entry event. The experience doesn't have to last long to make an impression. It might be a field trip to a location connected to the upcoming project, a visit from a guest speaker, a game or simulation, a compelling documentary, or another experience that fires up students' curiosity and gets them asking questions. As math teacher Telannia Norfar put it, a good entry event "captures students' hearts so their minds will follow."

The driving question offers another tool for engagement. By introducing the driving question when the project begins, you help frame the learning experience ahead. A good driving question should eliminate the all-too-common student question—"Why do we need to know this?"—by making the learning more purposeful.

With Bautista's voting project, for example, the driving question was *How can one vote affect my life and my community?* To answer that open-ended question, students asked many more need-to-know questions of their own. They conducted research into those questions and then applied their insights to produce public service announcements about why voting is important for a community.

Teachers typically introduce the driving question on the heels of an entry event, when curiosity is high. The right driving question will help students focus their inquiry, so it's important to phrase the question in student-friendly language or, even better, engage students in creating it together.

Sara Lev generated a driving question in collaboration with her transitional kindergarten students. She had learning goals in mind for the project, which focused on taking care of the environment, but she wanted to see if her young learners could generate their own driving question—with her help. She primed their thinking with an entry event. "I took photos of all the things that students had been complaining about recently—coats left on the floor, pencils unsharpened, things not being cared for in our environment. We looked at the photos and talked about what students noticed. Then we went for a walk around the school and talked about more observations when we came back. They noticed lots of examples of our environment not being taken care of. One student said, 'Why is this happening?' Another said, 'What can we do about it?' Those questions led us to our driving question: *How can we take care of the environment and inspire others to help us?*"

One sign of a good driving question is that it generates a cascade of need-to-know questions from students (see Figure 7.1).

Figure 7.1   Start with Inquiry

Want to Know
• Why are they only testing children/ toddlers?
• Does this happen anywhere else?
• How long does it take to fix the problem?
• How do the residents feel?
• What is being done?
• What are the lead levels of H_2O in NYC?
• What are the long-term effects of lead poisoning?
• Who is responsible?

Need to Know
• What are corrosive inhibitors?
• How do the pipes corrode?
• What is the impact of lead?
• Are they going to do something about the lead in the water?
• What is water (in chemistry)?
• Are corrosive inhibitors toxic?
• Do the lead strips work?
• Where is Flint?

Ray Ahmed's chemistry students launch into a new project by generating questions.

➲ Try This: Lead a Need-to-Know Discussion

Project Based Learning is fundamentally a process of sustained inquiry, which means students' work in a project is guided by questions. The questions should be generated by the students themselves. Right after an entry event and the introduction (or cocreation) of the driving question, the teacher facilitates a discussion about

◔ Try This: Lead a Need-to-Know Discussion (*continued*)

the questions students need to know in order to answer the driving question and successfully complete the project. There are several ways to do this, but here's the basic process:

1. Using a flip chart, whiteboard, or computer projector, write the heading "What do we need to know?" (*Optional:* Make it a two-column chart with one side labeled "What do we know?" and the other labeled "What do we need to know?" This allows you to activate students' prior knowledge of the topic.)

2. Give students the prompt and time to think and jot down ideas individually. Then meet in pairs or trios to brainstorm questions.

3. Lead a discussion (with you or a student recording notes) to create a list of questions, capturing students' exact words. Do not edit except for clarity, do not judge whether the questions are good or not, and do not answer the questions yet.

4. If you notice that students are not listing some important things you think they actually need to know for the project, try to elicit them by asking questions rather than putting your own ideas on the list. Students will have more chances to add to or revise the list as the project progresses. (*Optional:* Have students sort the questions into categories, such as "Open-Ended" and "Closed" or "Content, Process, and Product.")

5. Keep the list of questions visible or display it regularly during the project so it becomes a living document. When you revisit the list, put check marks next to the questions that have been answered. Add new questions as they arise, which will tend to get deeper as students learn more and dig into the topic and task. (Older students can manage this process themselves to some extent.)

Some PBL teachers add another column to the chart under the heading "How will we answer our questions?" They then lead a discussion or coach students to fill in this column independently.

You can also use the need-to-know list as a planning tool early in the project. Sort the questions into three categories—Content, Process, and Product—and then identify the lessons, experiences, materials, and resources (including experts) needed to address the questions.

Engage and Coach Through the Messy Middle

Many more opportunities to engage and coach emerge as the project unfolds. Like a sports coach, you size up the talents and skills of your "players" and plan learning activities that are just challenging enough to help each improve. You break complicated tasks and ideas into right-sized chunks or steps; scaffold the development of new skills; provide time to practice; and offer constructive, timely feedback. When students make gains or breakthroughs in understanding, you encourage them to reflect on their own growth and set new goals. You celebrate the small wins that will add up to deeper learning.

A coach is also good at reading the temperature of the room. You pay attention to how teams are getting along (or not) and step in when needed to help manage conflict. If students hit roadblocks, you help them learn from failure—and then recover. You know when they need a pep talk and when they need to vent their frustration.

"You can feel fatigue in the middle of a long project," says Erin Starkey, an instructional coach from Wichita Falls, Texas. If you know your students—a hallmark of a good coach—you'll be able to read the clues that engagement is flagging. That might be your signal to bring in an outside expert or plan field research to recharge interest in the project.

With elementary students, Starkey uses a project wall to keep artifacts visible. That includes students' questions. "The board becomes a focal point for students," she says. "When I know their questions, I can coach better." Eventually, she says, students start looking at one another's questions and working together to answer them. "They coach each other."

Even when students take the lead in designing their own projects, their interest can wane before they reach their goals. Chemistry teacher Ray Ahmed sometimes has to help students overcome a slump in the middle of extended inquiry projects. "It's exciting for them in the beginning, but after five weeks they might say, 'I'm tired of this! I'm sick of the question I came up with!'" The teacher coaches them through that challenge by reminding them that scientists often face the same problem. "That's a real-world issue," he admits. Successful scientists develop the perseverance to keep going through setbacks.

Ian Stevenson, director of school development at a high school in Memphis, Tennessee, sees the teacher's role as "coaching students to work as independently as possible throughout the process." A teacher as coach should be able to "identify what students need and provide them with resources, encouragement, and redirection as you guide them through the project."

A good coach also knows when to step back and let students lead. "For me," Stevenson says, "engagement is when students are actively talking about content and making sense of it. When that's happening, I need to shut up and let them talk!"

If you notice that students are not driving their own learning, however, you may need to deliberately build the skills of self-management. We heard earlier how Telannia Norfar intervened when she saw her students struggling to work semi-independently. She took back the reins—for a while—and supported students' self-management skills with daily task logs. Over time, as students developed better work habits, she was able to gradually release more of the responsibility to them.

The teacher as coach not only celebrates small wins but also reengages students who are struggling or straggling. Effective formative assessment (discussed in Chapter 5) helps you identify when students need support—and why. Scaffolding strategies (discussed in Chapter 6) ensure that you are helping all students reach learning goals. An effective PBL teacher knows how to move seamlessly from formative assessment to just-in-time scaffolding.

For example, high school teacher Brian Schoch from Columbus, Ohio, was off and running with a promising project. His business students appeared to be fully engaged in the challenge of designing products that they would market to an audience of 4th graders. Previously, they had researched existing products in their price range and interviewed 4th graders who served as their focus group. Now they were at the stage in the project when it was time for teams to brainstorm product ideas.

As he circulated around the room, Schoch could tell from the conversations that some teams were fully invested in the challenge. "If I heard them brainstorming and suggesting different strategies, I would hang back." But when he noticed one table where students sat slumped and quiet, struggling to get their creativity flowing, he pulled up a chair and started asking questions.

"What have you tried? What do you remember from talking with the fourth graders? What were your favorite things when you were their age?" His questions were intended to prompt students' thinking, but he stopped short of offering specific ideas for products. "I didn't want them to create something they thought I would like. The ideas had to come from them," he said.

He also reminded teammates of their goal, defined by the driving question: *How can we design a product to appeal to our target audience of 4th graders?* After just a few minutes of Schoch's friendly but deliberate questioning, the group was refocused and generating ideas. The teacher quietly moved on. His teacher moves were quick and effective: listening and observing for evidence of engagement, using open-ended questions to help students get unstuck, encouraging persistence, and helping students refocus on their learning goal.

With practice and reflection, Project Based Teachers become adept at holding students to high standards while still showing care and concern for their struggles. They take on the role of a "warm demander," a term used by MacArthur Award–winning educator and equity advocate Lisa Delpit (2012). She describes warm demanders as teachers who "expect a great deal of their students, convince them of their own brilliance, and help them to reach their potential in a disciplined and structured environment" (p. 77). Figure 7.2 describes warm demander behaviors, with prompts to consider how to emphasize them in your teaching practice.

Figure 7.2   Warm Demander Behaviors

Reflection on Practice		
Warm Demander Behaviors	How do I already do this?	How can I build on this?
Build trust		
Show warmth and care for my students		
Learn about my students and their lives		
Hold and communicate high academic and cognitive standards for all of my students		
Differentiate scaffolding to encourage and support "productive struggle"		

Reflection prompts encourage teachers to consider their use of "warm demander" behaviors.

When students are building understanding and brainstorming product ideas, apply your "coaching stance" to reinforce a classroom culture of high expectations. Use your project rubric as a focus for coaching conversations about students' learning goals. Ask questions that help students assess their own progress and work toward excellence. When students are working on products, for example, coach them to take a critical look at their work in progress. Ask questions such as "Is your work good enough? Where would you describe your learning on the rubric today?" These questions facilitate students' engagement and get them thinking about their own learning. That's a powerful tool.

Celebrate and Reflect at the Finish Line

As a project comes to a close, teachers continue in their coaching role by celebrating students' accomplishments and helping them reflect on their progress. You have likely encouraged reflection throughout the project, but now is the time for a final meta-moment. Encourage students to pause and take stock of their extended learning experience. How have they wrestled with challenges, gained confidence, and surprised themselves (and others) with their results? Did their culminating event or product lead to the desired outcomes? Did they make a difference? What are the new goals they want to tackle in the next project?

This is also time to ask students to reflect on the project itself. Would they recommend changes if you use the same plan again? Where were the weak spots? Can they pinpoint specific learning activities or scaffolds that were critical to their success? By inviting students to critique your work as project designer, you are inviting them to put on their own coaching hat and offer you some useful feedback to support your continuing growth as a Project Based Teacher.

Coaches' Notebook: Asking the Right Questions

Instructional coaches play a unique role in schools that are shifting to PBL. They aren't evaluators of teacher performance, and they aren't administrators. "It's all about creating a relationship with teachers—just like in a PBL classroom, where the relationship between teacher and students is so important," says Ian Stevenson, who coaches teachers as part of his role at a Memphis, Tennessee, high school.

Questioning is at the heart of instructional coaching—once again, mirroring how inquiry drives learning in PBL. The right questions can help an instructional coach identify which goals to work on with teachers to support them in adopting PBL practices.

Here are some of Stevenson's go-to questions to start the coaching process with teachers:

What got you into teaching? This question works with new teachers and experienced teachers. They all have a story. Later on, once Project Based Learning starts to work for them, they'll often say it reminds them of why they started teaching in the first place.

What is it about PBL that attracts you? This question gives you insights about their motivation. If I know what they're passionate about, it's easier to engage in the work of helping them change some of their teaching practices. Their answers offer insights about which roads to follow with them.

What do you think you do well? This question allows me to approach coaching from a growth mindset. If we start with what they do well, we can work toward what they might do better. Maybe they're good at building routines in the classroom, so class management is not a problem. Great. We can start there and think about adding routines that better support a PBL classroom.

What do you want me to focus on with you? This gets us to a more specific goal. It's all driven by what the teacher wants to work on. Then I can offer to make observations, model a lesson, gather data, interview students—all in support of that teacher's goal.

At the end of a coaching cycle, just as at the end of a project, "I get to be the cheerleader," Stevenson adds. "Sometimes, teachers don't recognize the progress they're making. It's part of my job as a coach to point out their successes and celebrate them."

Strategies to Engage and Coach: Key Takeaways

In this chapter, you read about many ways to engage and coach students in PBL, along with examples of engaging and coaching in action. Take time to reflect on your current practices as you consider strategies to improve your approach to engaging and coaching in PBL.

- How comfortable are you with adopting the teacher-as-coach role? How is coaching different from the traditional role of a teacher?

- How have you engaged students at project launch in the past? What are the signs you look for to know that students are engaged?
- During the messy middle of a project, how have you coached students to overcome challenges or keep going if their interest starts to flag?
- At the end of a project, how do you encourage students to reflect on their growth? How do you celebrate successes in learning?

On Your PBL Bookshelf

The Art of Coaching: Effective Strategies for School Transformation: Rather than focusing on classroom strategies to engage and coach students, Elena Aguilar addresses instructional coaching. Her insights are useful for teacher leaders, instructional coaches, and PBL mentors looking for practical ways to support teachers as they adopt new strategies for teaching and learning.

Cultivating Curiosity in K–12 Classrooms: How to Promote and Sustain Deep Learning: Wendy Ostroff explains how teachers can transform students' natural curiosity into deep inquiry through careful listening, thoughtful facilitation, deliberate strategies for engagement, and learning alongside students.

Learning for Keeps: Teaching the Strategies Essential for Creating Independent Learners: Rhoda Koenig recommends strategies for "skating alongside" students as they develop the competencies and independence to succeed on their own. Her practical coaching strategies for gradually releasing control of learning to students and fostering their self-direction align nicely with PBT practices.

Teaching in the Fast Lane: How to Create Active Learning Experiences: Suzy Pepper Rollins debunks the myth that student-centered learning is an unstructured free-for-all. Instead, she makes the case for intentional teaching practices that put students in an active learning mode—collaborating, engaging with content, thinking critically, and taking more responsibility for their own learning.

8

Closing Reflections

Reflecting on your practice is key to improving at Project Based Teaching.

The educators you've met in the previous chapters developed their expertise with Project Based Teaching in different ways. Some were part of schoolwide shifts to PBL. Many were PBL pioneers in their buildings or districts, eager to find a better way to make education more engaging and meaningful for their students. A few had the chance to experience PBL during their preservice training, or even earlier.

Whatever their starting point, they all agree that PBL gets better with practice. Becoming a skilled Project Based Teacher doesn't happen with one project. It's an ongoing process of professional learning and reflection, supported by effective school leaders, instructional coaches, and teaching colleagues.

⊙ Try This: Reflect on Your Project

Shortly after a project concludes, take time to record some thoughts on how it went. Use your students' comments about it and any other data—such as student work, feedback from other adults involved in the project, and assessment results—to inform your reflection. Your conclusions will help you improve the project for next time or plan future projects with the lessons learned in mind.

Here are some types of questions to ask yourself, plus some examples:

- **Content:** Were the standards and other learning goals you selected appropriate for the project? Were there too many, or too few, and could others have been included? If you involved experts in the project, what did they think (assuming you asked them) about what students should learn—and were there other aspects of the topic they thought would have been good to include?

- **Project design:** Was it a good topic for PBL? Did the project engage students? Did it include effective use of all of the Gold Standard PBL Essential Project Design Elements, to some extent? Were the entry event and driving question effective? Were the final products a good choice for students to demonstrate understanding? Was it the right length of time?

- **Teaching:** Were there some Project Based Teaching Practices you felt better at than others? How could you learn more or enhance your practice in those areas for the next time you do a project?

- **Results:** Did students adequately learn and develop key knowledge, understanding, and success skills? Was their work of high quality? If not, how could it have been improved? Were there additional outcomes of the project that surprised or pleased you?

Let's close with a few final reflections that may help you on your own PBL journey. Primary teacher Sara Lev revels in projects "that stretch my students—and me." Although she has taught only with PBL throughout her entire teaching career, she still gets butterflies at the start of every new project experience. "I start with some anxiety. My husband reminds me that I say this every time! It's a little unsettling because I don't know exactly what's going to happen. But that's the exciting part of teaching. You hand over the ownership to students, and their level of engagement is so high. The students get behind it, then the parents get behind it. And somehow, it usually all works out."

Middle school history teacher Tom Neville recalls an experience from earlier in his career that convinced him PBL is worth the effort. His first foray into PBL was at a school where traditional teaching was the norm. The culture was not conducive to student inquiry or teacher innovation.

Neville recounts what happened in his first project, which challenged students to chronicle the history of a Washington, DC, alley and share their findings with an audience of historians and preservationists. "The students explained that this shift to Project Based Learning was not desirable for them at the start, underscoring the fact that the larger culture of the school was not exactly inclined to work in this way. They didn't want projects. They wanted what they had become capable of doing well enough: lectures and tests. They even met outside of class to discuss it and designate a leader to confront me in class and say, verbatim: 'We want you to lecture and test us.'"

By the end of the project, however, the same student who had led the opposition became an outspoken advocate for PBL. Neville continues, "Granted, my work at the start of that year could have been much better, but it required taking the risk of moving in that direction, sticking with that direction despite doubts and stumbles, being open and honest in dialogue with students about these decisions and ideas along the way, and finding ways to connect beyond the classroom to make the work more meaningful in ways that helped to compensate for my shortcomings and inexperience with this pedagogy."

Neville has since changed schools and is now in a context that supports PBL. Nevertheless, he continues experimenting, reflecting, and fine-tuning "to figure out the best way to balance time, assessment, and scaffolding." His message to teaching colleagues? "It would be unfair for us to increasingly emphasize to our students the importance of experimentation, risk taking, and the lessons in failure if we don't operate on the same mindset in our own work."

For high school teacher Ray Ahmed, PBL has become a way to connect his students' lives to academic content in deeply meaningful ways. "When you're doing chemistry as a career, you're not just sitting in a lab. You're actually applying it to restore buildings, make sure water is safe, and so forth," he says. A project that focused on the Flint, Michigan, water crisis, for example, "is about an event that happened to real people that caused tremendous harm." Although chemistry was part of the problem, it also offered solutions. "It was important for my students to see how chemistry can be used responsibly from different perspectives in the real world."

Ahmed's use of outside experts also expanded students' awareness of how people attempt to address real problems. "The experts were not only chemists but people who are activists, people involved in social policy. This mirrors what I hope emanates from a project—that we learn something from each other, and that every member of the team is important. They all have something to contribute."

Finally, some practical advice from high school teacher Erin Brandvold. She recalls a moment, early in her career, when a project exhibition was coming up to showcase student work. She wasn't sure students would be ready for showtime. "I was freaking out," she admits. A colleague who was more seasoned in PBL offered some advice that stuck with her. "He said, 'If you want to do PBL, you just have to jump in.'" She took his advice, despite her doubts, and students rose to the occasion.

For school leaders who are supporting their teachers' growth with PBL, here's one more idea to borrow from a PBL veteran.

At the end of every class period, Brandvold finds something specific to compliment about her students' efforts. "I tell them something I appreciated about them that day. Little things like that make students feel seen. They know their hard work is valued. That makes them more comfortable taking risks or investing that extra effort."

Just like Brandvold's students, teachers who are new to PBL need encouragement for their efforts. They need to feel comfortable taking risks. They need opportunities to get constructive feedback and time to apply that feedback to make revisions.

Project Based Learning is all about learning by doing. Not surprisingly, the same holds true for Project Based Teaching. It's through *doing PBL*—and reflecting on your experience—that you'll master the Project Based Teaching Practices.

Appendix

Project Based Teaching Rubric

Project Based Teaching Practice	Beginning PBL Teacher	Developing PBL Teacher	Gold Standard PBL Teacher
Build the Culture	• Norms are created to guide project work, but they may still feel like "rules" imposed and monitored by the teacher. • Students are asked for their ideas and given some choices to make, but opportunities for student voice and choice are infrequent or are only related to minor matters. • Students occasionally work independently but often look to the teacher for guidance. • Student teams are often unproductive or require frequent intervention by the teacher. • Students feel like there is a "right answer" they are supposed to give, rather than asking their own questions and arriving at their own answers; they are fearful of making mistakes. • Value is placed on "getting it done," and time is not allowed for revision of work; "coverage" is emphasized over quality and depth.	• Norms to guide the classroom are cocrafted with students, and students are beginning to internalize these norms. • Student voice and choice is encouraged through intentionally designed opportunities (e.g., when choosing teams, finding resources, using critique protocols, creating products). • Students work independently to some extent but look to the teacher for direction more often than necessary. • Student teams are generally productive and are learning what it means to move from cooperation to effective collaboration; teacher occasionally has to intervene or manage their work. • Students understand there is more than one way to answer a driving question and complete the project but are still cautious about proposing and testing ideas in case they are perceived to be "wrong." • The values of critique and revision, persistence, rigorous	• Norms to guide the classroom are cocrafted with and self-monitored by students. • Student voice and choice is regularly leveraged and ongoing, including identification of real-world issues and problems students want to address in projects. • Students usually know what they need to do with minimal direction from the teacher. • Students work collaboratively in healthy, high-functioning teams, much like an authentic work environment; the teacher rarely needs to be involved in managing teams. • Students understand there is no single "right answer" or preferred way to do the project and that it is OK to take risks, make mistakes, and learn from them. • The values of critique and revision, persistence, rigorous thinking, and pride in doing high-quality work are shared, and students hold one another accountable to them.

Project Based Teaching Practice	Beginning PBL Teacher	Developing PBL Teacher	Gold Standard PBL Teacher
Build the Culture— (*continued*)		• thinking, and pride in doing high-quality work are promoted by the teacher but not yet owned by students.	
Design and Plan	• Project includes some Essential Project Design Elements, but not at the highest level of the project design rubric. • Plans for scaffolding and assessing student learning lack some detail; project calendar needs more detail or is not followed. • Some resources for the project have not been anticipated or arranged in advance.	• Project includes all Essential Project Design Elements, but some are not at the highest level of the project design rubric. • Plans for scaffolding and assessing student learning lack some details; the project calendar allows too much or too little time, or it is followed too rigidly to respond to student needs. • Most resources for the project have been anticipated and arranged in advance.	• Project includes all Essential Project Design Elements as described on the project design rubric. • Plans are detailed and include scaffolding and assessment of student learning and a project calendar, which remains flexible to meet student needs. • Resources for the project have been anticipated to the fullest extent possible and arranged well in advance.
Align to Standards	• Criteria for products are given but are not specifically derived from standards. • Scaffolding of student learning, critique and revision protocols, assessments, and rubrics do not refer to or support student achievement of specific standards.	• Criteria for some products are not specified clearly enough to provide evidence that students have met all targeted standards. • Scaffolding of student learning, critique and revision protocols, assessments, and rubrics do not always refer to or support student achievement of specific standards.	• Criteria for products are clearly and specifically derived from standards and allow demonstration of mastery. • Scaffolding of student learning, critique and revision protocols, assessments, and rubrics consistently refer to and support student achievement of specific standards.

Manage Activities	• The classroom features some individual and team work time and small-group instruction, but too much time is given to whole-group instruction. • Either teams are formed using a random process (e.g., counting off) or students are allowed to form their own teams with no formal criteria or process. • Classroom routines and norms for project work time are not clearly established; time is not used productively. • Schedules, checkpoints, and deadlines are set, but they are loosely followed or unrealistic; bottlenecks impede workflow.	• The classroom features individual and team work time and whole-group and small-group instruction, but these structures are not well balanced throughout the project. • Generally well-balanced teams are formed but without considering the specific nature of the project; students have too much voice and choice in the process or not enough. • Classroom routines and norms are established for project work time but are not consistently followed; productivity is variable. • Realistic schedules, checkpoints, and deadlines are set, but more flexibility is needed; bottlenecks sometimes occur.	• The classroom features an appropriate mixture of individual and team work time, including both whole-group and small-group instruction. • Well-balanced teams are formed according to the nature of the project and student needs, with appropriate student voice and choice. • Project management tools (group calendar, team contracts, learning logs, and so forth) are used to support student self-management and independence, as well as collaboration. • Classroom routines and norms are consistently followed during project work time to maximize productivity. • Realistic schedules, checkpoints, and deadlines are set but flexible; no bottlenecks impede workflow.
Assess Student Learning	• Student learning of subject-area standards is assessed mainly through traditional means, such as a test, rather than products; success skills are not assessed. • Team-created products are used to assess student learning, making it difficult to assess whether individual students have met standards.	• Project products and other sources of evidence are used to assess subject-area standards; success skills are assessed to some extent. • Individual student learning—not just team-created products—is assessed to some extent, but the teacher lacks adequate evidence of individual student mastery.	• Project products and other sources of evidence are used to thoroughly assess subject-area standards as well as success skills. • Individual student learning—not just team-created products—is adequately assessed. • Formative assessment is used regularly and frequently with a variety of tools and processes.

Project Based Teaching Practice	Beginning PBL Teacher	Developing PBL Teacher	Gold Standard PBL Teacher
Assess Student Learning (continued)	• Formative assessment is used occasionally but not regularly or with a variety of tools and processes. • Protocols for critique and revision are not used, or they are informal; feedback is superficial or not used to improve work. • Students assess their own work informally, but the teacher does not provide regular, structured opportunities to do so. • Rubrics are used to assess final products but not as a formative tool; rubrics are not derived from standards.	• Formative assessment is used on several occasions, using a few different tools and processes. • Structured protocols for critique and revision and other formative assessment techniques are used occasionally; students are learning how to give and use feedback. • Opportunities are provided for students to self-assess their progress, but they are too unstructured or infrequent. • Standards-aligned rubrics are used by the teacher to guide both formative and summative assessment.	• Structured protocols for critique and revision are used regularly at checkpoints; students give and receive effective feedback to inform instructional decisions and students' actions. • Regular, structured opportunities are provided for students to self-assess their progress and, when appropriate, assess peers on their performance. • Standards-aligned rubrics are used by students and the teacher throughout the project to guide both formative and summative assessment.
Scaffold Student Learning	• Students receive some instructional supports to access both content and resources, but many individual needs are not met. • The teacher may front-load content knowledge before the project launch, instead of waiting for need-to-know points during the project. • Students gain key success skills as a side effect of the project, but they are not taught intentionally.	• Most students receive instructional supports to access both content and resources, but some individual needs are not met. • Scaffolding is guided to some extent by students' questions and need-to-knows, but some of it may still be front-loaded. • Key success skills are taught, but students need more opportunities to practice success skills before applying them.	• Each student receives necessary instructional supports to access content, skills, and resources; these supports are removed when no longer needed. • Scaffolding is guided as much as possible by students' questions and needs; the teacher does not front-load too much information at the start of the project but waits until it is needed or requested by students.

	• Students are asked to do research or gather data but without adequate guidance; deeper questions are not generated based on information gathered.	• Student inquiry is facilitated and scaffolded, but more is needed; teacher may overdirect the process and limit independent thinking by students.	• Key success skills are taught using a variety of tools and strategies; students are provided with opportunities to practice and apply them, and then reflect on progress. • Student inquiry is facilitated and scaffolded, while allowing students to act and think as independently as possible.
Engage and Coach	• The teacher has some knowledge of students' strengths, interests, backgrounds, and lives, but it does not significantly affect instructional decision making. • Project goals are developed without seeking student input. • Students are willing to do the project as if it were another assignment, but the teacher does not create a sense of ownership or fuel motivation. • The driving question is presented at the project launch and student questions are generated, but they are not used to guide inquiry or product development.	• The teacher has a general knowledge of students' strengths, interests, backgrounds, and lives and considers it when teaching the project. • Project goals and benchmarks are set with some input from students. • Students are excited by the project and motivated to work hard by the teacher's enthusiasm and commitment to their success. • Students' questions guide inquiry to some extent, but some are answered too quickly by the teacher; students occasionally reflect on the driving question.	• The teacher's knowledge of individual student strengths, interests, backgrounds, and lives is used to engage them in the project and inform instructional decision making. • Students and teacher use standards to codefine goals and benchmarks for the project in developmentally appropriate ways (e.g., by constructing a rubric together). • Students' enthusiasm for and sense of ownership of the project is maintained by the shared nature of the work between teachers and students.

Project Based Teaching Practice	Beginning PBL Teacher	Developing PBL Teacher	Gold Standard PBL Teacher
Engage and Coach (continued)	• Expectations for the performance of all students are not clear, too low, or too high. • There is limited relationship building in the classroom, resulting in student needs that are not identified or addressed. • Students and the teacher informally reflect on what (content) and how (process) students are learning; reflection occurs mainly at the end of the project.	• Appropriately high expectations for the performance of all students are set and communicated by the teacher. • Student needs for further instruction or practice, additional resources, redirection, troubleshooting, praise, encouragement, and celebration are identified through relationship building and close observation and interaction. • Students and the teacher occasionally reflect on what (content) and how (process) students are learning.	• Student questions play the central role in driving the inquiry and product development process; the driving question is actively used to sustain inquiry. • Appropriately high expectations for the performance of all students are clearly established, shared, and reinforced by teachers and students. • Individual student needs are identified through close relationships built with the teacher; needs are met not only by the teacher but by students themselves or other students, acting independently. • Students and teacher reflect regularly and formally throughout the project on what (content) and how (process) students are learning; they specifically note and celebrate gains and accomplishments.

Student Learning Guide

NOTE: The following Student Learning Guide was developed by teacher Erin Brandvold for the high school world history project Revolutions on Trial. Blank versions of the Student Learning Guide can be downloaded at www. bie.org/object/document/project_design_overview_and_student_learning_guide.

Project Design: Student Learning Guide

Project: Revolutions on Trial

Driving Question: How can we, as historians, determine the effectiveness of a revolution in improving the lives of citizens?

Final Product(s) Presentations, Performances, Products and/or Services	Learning Outcomes/Targets knowledge, understanding & success skills needed by students to successfully complete products	Checkpoints/Formative Assessment to check for learning and ensure students are on track	Instructional Strategies for All Learners provided by teacher, other staff, experts; includes scaffolds, materials, lessons aligned to learning outcomes and formative assessment
(Individual) **Weeks 1–3** Pretrial Timed Write in which students present their argument and supporting evidence to be used in the trial	I can explain how a revolution starts, using the Revolution Framework, and apply that framework to Nation X and the Mexican, Haitian, or Cuban revolution.	• Framework quiz • Nation X Reflection • Comparison between Nation X framework and chosen revolution framework	• Direct instruction about framework • Jigsaw creation of Nation X framework • Summaries of revolutions with annotations to identify the elements of the framework

	I can…	Assessment	Strategies
	I can determine the criteria for evaluating the effectiveness of a revolution.	• Evaluating Nation X using cocreated criteria	• Small-group discussions defining *effectiveness* and creating a list of criteria • Whole-group consolidation of list
(Individual) **Weeks 1–3** Pretrial Timed Write in which students present their argument and supporting evidence to be used in the trial—*(continued)*	I can use primary and secondary sources to gather evidence about a revolution.	• SOAPS quiz • Creation of four source cards (two primary/two secondary) with evidence • Evidence gallery walk with time for revision	• Primary/secondary source packets provided about revolutionaries' lives and motives • Primary and secondary source packets about prerevolutionary governments • Primary/secondary source packets with documents about citizens' lives both pre- and post-revolution • Source Card review (SOAPS for sourcing evidence) • Quality criteria for evidence (accurate, substantial, and varied)
	I can use evidence to support an argument about a revolution. I can identify counterarguments and use them to strengthen my own argument.	• Argument gallery walk with time for revision • Peer review of argument/evidence connections	• Quality Criteria for a precise argument • Use of revolution criteria to select evidence and create arguments

Project Design: Student Learning Guide (*continued*)

	I can analyze the motives behind revolutionaries' actions.	• Revolutionary Witnesses create a Witness Affidavit to summarize their role and motives in the revolution • Teacher feedback on witness profiles • Lawyers create a Witness Brief to show their interpretation of witnesses' motives • Legal expert feedback on Witness Brief	• Legal Expert interviews about how to prepare as a witness and a lawyer to defend or prosecute your case • Case Theory creation for students to identify argument, evidence, and counterarguments and the links between them • Collaboration protocol to teams to use source cards to create Witness Affidavits and witness briefs • Graphic organizers for witness profiles and witness briefs
(Team) **Week 4** Mock Trial Case Theory	I can analyze the effects of dictatorships and subsequent revolutions on their people.	• Government Witnesses create a Witness Affidavit to summarize their leadership • Teacher feedback on witness profiles • Citizen Witnesses create a Witness Affidavit to summarize their pre-revolutionary lives • Legal expert feedback on witness briefs	

(Individual) **Weeks 5–6** Mock Trial Participation	I can determine the effectiveness of revolutions in improving the lives of citizens.	• Exit tickets throughout creation and rehearsal time reflecting on the facts of the trial • Whole-class discussion after mock trial: Which side actually should have won?	• Final verdict predictions • Warm-ups and exit tickets throughout trial prep • Discussion questions prepped in advance
	I can use probing questions to demonstrate my interpretation of revolutionaries' motives	• Peer rehearsal and feedback • Graded question lists • Teacher feedback on rehearsals	• Watch and evaluate trial videos • Sort questions into types and practice creating deeper probing questions • Quick-fire drills for asking and answering impromptu question • Expert interviews
	I can use professional presentation skills to effectively communicate my ideas to my audience.	• Peer rehearsal and feedback • Teacher feedback on rehearsals	• Create quality criteria for professional presentation skills • Watch and evaluate trial videos • Expert interviews: What does it look/sound like to be in a courtroom?

References

Aguilar, E. (2013). *The art of coaching: Effective strategies for school transformation.* San Francisco: Jossey-Bass.

Ainsworth, L. (2013). *Prioritizing the Common Core: Identifying specific standards to emphasize the most.* Boston: Houghton Mifflin Harcourt.

Ainsworth, L. (2014a). *Power standards: Identifying the standards that matter the most.* Boston: Houghton Mifflin Harcourt.

Ainsworth, L. (2014b). *Prioritizing the common core: Identifying specific standards to emphasize the most.* Boston: Houghton Mifflin Harcourt.

Alber, R. (2014, January 24). 6 scaffolding strategies to use with your students [blog post]. Retrieved from *Edutopia* at www.edutopia.org/blog/scaffolding-lessons-six-strategies-rebecca-alber

Beard, A. (2015, October). Life's work: An interview with Andre Agassi. *Harvard Business Review.* Retrieved from https://hbr.org/2015/10/andre-agassi

Benson, B. (1997). Scaffolding (coming to terms). *English Journal, 86*(7), 126–127.

Berger, R. (2003). *An ethic of excellence: Building a culture of craftsmanship with students.* Portsmouth, NH: Heinemann.

Berger, R., Rugan, L., & Woodfin, L. (2014). *Leaders of their own learning: Transforming schools through student-engaged assessment.* San Francisco: Jossey-Bass.

Boss, S. (2013). *PBL for 21st century success.* Novato, CA: Buck Institute for Education.

Boss, S. (2015). *Real-world projects: How do I design relevant and engaging learning experiences?* Alexandria, VA: ASCD.

Boss, S., & Krauss, J. (in press). *Reinventing project-based learning: Your field guide to real-world projects in the digital age* (3rd ed.). Eugene, OR: International Society for Technology in Education.

Brookhart, S. (2013). *How to create and use rubrics for formative assessment and grading*. Alexandria, VA: ASCD.

Burns, M. (2018). *Tasks before apps: Designing rigorous learning in a tech-rich classroom*. Alexandria, VA: ASCD.

Çakiroğlu, Ü., Akkan, Y., & Güven, B. (2012). Analyzing the effect of web-based instruction applications to school culture within technology integration. *Educational Sciences: Theory and Practice, 12,* 1043–1048.

Chappuis, J., & Stiggins, R. (2011). *An introduction to student-involved assessment FOR learning*. New York: Pearson.

Deal, T. E., & Peterson, K. D. (2009). *Shaping school culture: Pitfalls, paradoxes, and promises* (2nd ed.). San Francisco: Jossey-Bass.

Delpit, L. (2012). *Multiplication is for white people: Raising expectations for other people's children*. New York: New Press.

DeWitt, P., & Slade, S. (2014). *School climate change: How do I build a positive environment for learning?* Alexandria, VA: ASCD.

Doubet, K., & Hockett, J. (2015). *Differentiation in middle and high school: Strategies to engage all learners*. Alexandria, VA: ASCD.

Doubet, K., & Hockett, J. (2017). *Differentiation in the elementary grades: Strategies to engage and equip all learners*. Alexandria, VA: ASCD.

Duhigg, C. (2016, Febraury 25). What Google learned from its quest to build the perfect team. *New York Times Magazine*. Retrieved from www.nytimes.com/2016/02/28/magazine/what-google-learned-from-its-quest-to-build-the-perfect-team.html

Fester, J. (2017, April 26). Interdisciplinary projects: 3 protocols for curricular connections [blog post]. Retrieved from *PBL Blog, Buck Institute for Education* at www.bie.org/blog/interdisciplinary_projects_3_protocols_for_finding_curricular_connections

Finley, T. (2014, August 12). The science behind classroom norming [blog post]. Retrieved from *Edutopia* at www.edutopia.org/blog/establishing-classroom-norms-todd-finley

Fisher, D., & Frey, N. (2011). *The formative assessment action plan: Practical steps to more successful teaching and learning*. Alexandria, VA: ASCD.

Fisher, D., Frey, N., & Hite, S. A. (2016). *Intentional and targeted teaching: A framework for teacher growth and leadership*. Alexandria, VA: ASCD.

Fisher, D., Frey, N., & Pumpian, I. (2012). *How to create a culture of achievement in your school and classroom*. Alexandria, VA: ASCD.

Fletcher, A. (2002). *FireStarter youth power curriculum: Participant guidebook*. Olympia, WA: Freechild Project.

Gant, K. (2017, January 30). What to do during student work time [blog post]. Retrieved from *Intrepid ED: Exploring the Landscape of PBL and Instruction* at https://intrepidedblog.wordpress.com/2017/01/30/what-to-do-during-student-work-time

Hallerman, S., & Larmer, J. (2011). *PBL in the elementary grades: Step-by-step guidance, tools and tips for standards-focused K–5 projects.* Novato, CA: Buck Institute for Education.

Hammond, Z. (2014). *Culturally responsive teaching and the brain: Promoting authentic engagement and rigor among culturally and linguistically diverse students.* Thousand Oaks, CA: Corwin.

Jackson, R. (2009). *Never work harder than your students and other principles of great teaching.* Alexandria, VA: ASCD.

Jerald, C. D. (2006, December). School culture: "The hidden curriculum." *Issue Brief.* Washington, DC: Center for Comprehensive School Reform and Improvement. Retrieved from http://files.eric.ed.gov/fulltext/ED495013.pdf

Jobs for the Future & the Council of Chief State School Officers. (2015). *Educator competencies for personalized, learner-centered teaching.* Boston: Jobs for the Future.

Kallick, B., & Zmuda, A. (2016). *Students at the center: Personalized learning with habits of mind.* Alexandria, VA: ASCD.

Kane, L., Hoff, N., Cathcart, A., Heifner, A., Palmon, S., & Peterson, R. L. (2016, February). *School climate and culture.* Strategy brief. Lincoln, NE: Student Engagement Project, University of Nebraska–Lincoln and the Nebraska Department of Education.

Koenig, R. (2010). *Learning for keeps: Teaching the strategies essential for creating independent learners.* Alexandria, VA: ASCD.

Larmer, J. (2017). *PBL starter kit: To-the-point advice, tools and tips for your first project in middle or high school* (2nd ed.). Novato, CA: Buck Institute for Education.

Larmer, J., Mergendoller, J., & Boss, S. (2015). *Setting the standard for Project Based Learning: A proven approach to rigorous classroom instruction.* Alexandria, VA: ASCD.

Laur, D., & Ackers, J. (2017). *Developing natural curiosity through project-based learning: Five strategies for the PreK–3 classroom.* New York: Routledge.

Lemov, D. (2015). *Teach like a champion 2.0: 62 techniques that put students on the path to college.* San Francisco: Jossey-Bass.

Macarelli, K. (2010). *Teaching science with interactive notebooks.* Thousand Oaks, CA: Corwin.

Mattoon, M. (2015, Spring). *What are protocols? Why use them?* National School Reform Faculty. Retrieved from www.nsrfharmony.org/system/files/protocols/WhatAreProtocols%2BWhyUse_0.pdf

McCarthy, J. (2017). *So all can learn: A practical guide to differentiation.* Lanham, MD: Rowman & Littlefield.

McDowell, M. (2017). *Rigorous PBL by design: Three shifts for developing confident and competent learners.* Thousand Oaks, CA: Corwin.

Miller, A. (2017, March 30). 7 tips for coaching PBL teachers [blog post]. Retrieved from *PBL Blog, Buck Institute for Education* at www.bie.org/blog/7_tips_for_coaching_pbl_teachers

Moss, C., & Brookhart, S. (2012). *Learning targets: Helping students aim for understanding in today's lesson.* Alexandria, VA: ASCD.

Olson, K. (2014, March 1). Teacher as coach: Transforming teaching with a coaching mindset [blog post]. Retrieved from *Pedagogies of Abundance* at https://oldsow.wordpress.com/2014/03/01/teacher-as-coach-transforming-teaching-with-the-a-coaching-mindset

Ostroff, W. (2016). *Cultivating curiosity in K–12 classrooms: How to promote and sustain deep learning.* Alexandria, VA: ASCD.

Palmer, E. (2011). *Well spoken: Teaching speaking to all students.* Portland, ME: Stenhouse.

Project Management Institute Educational Foundation. (2016). *Project management toolkit for teachers.* Newtown Square, PA: Author. Retrieved from https://pmief.org/library/resources/project-management-toolkit-for-teachers

Project Zero. (n.d.). Visible thinking. Retrieved from www.visiblethinkingpz.org/VisibleThinking_html_files/VisibleThinking1.html

Rebora, A. (2008, September 10). Making a difference: Carol Ann Tomlinson explains how differentiated instruction works and why we need it now [blog post]. Retrieved from *Education Week: Teacher PD Sourcebook* at www.edweek.org/tsb/articles/2008/09/10/01tomlinson.h02.html

Rindone, N. K. (1996). Effective teaming for success. Presented at the workshop for the Kansas State Department of Education, Students Support Services, Boots Adams Alumni Center, University of Kansas, Lawrence, KS.

Ritchhart, R. (2015). *Creating cultures of thinking: The 8 forces we must master to truly transform our schools.* San Francisco: Jossey-Bass.

Rollins, S. (2017). *Teaching in the fast lane: How to create active learning experiences.* Alexandria, VA: ASCD.

Rothstein, D., & Santana, L. (2011). *Make just one change: Teach students to ask their own questions.* Cambridge, MA: Harvard Education Press.

Sackstein, S. (2017). *Peer feedback in the classroom: Empowering students to be the experts.* Alexandria, VA: ASCD.

Scott, D., & Marzano, R. J. (2014). *Awaken the learner: Finding the source of effective education.* Bloomington, IN: Marzano Research Laboratory.

Scriven, M. S. (1991). *Evaluation thesaurus* (4th ed.). Newbury Park, CA: Sage.

Searle, M. (2013). *Causes and cures in the classroom: Getting to the root of academic and behavior problems.* Alexandria, VA: ASCD.

Sizer, T. (2004). *Horace's compromise: The dilemma of the American high school.* New York: Mariner.

Slade, S. (2014, June 17). Classroom culture: It's your decision [blog post]. Retrieved from *ASCD InService* at http://inservice.ascd.org/classroom-culture-its-your-decision

Steele, D., & Cohn-Vargas, B. (2013). *Identity safe classrooms: Places to belong and learn.* Thousand Oaks, CA: Corwin.

Stiggins, R. (2007, May). Assessment through the student's eyes. *Educational Leadership, 64*(8), 22–26.

Tomlinson, C. A. (2011). One to grow on: Every teacher a coach. *Educational Leadership, 69*(2), 92–93.

Tomlinson, C. A. (2017). *How to differentiate instruction in academically diverse classrooms* (3rd ed.). Alexandria, VA: ASCD.

Tomlinson, C. A., & Allen, S. (2000). *Leadership for differentiating schools and classrooms.* Alexandria, VA: ASCD.

Uliasz, K. (2016, April 13). Inclusive special education via PBL [blog post]. Retrieved from *PBL Blog. Buck Institute for Education* at www.bie.org/blog/inclusive_special_education_via_pbl

Werberger, R. (2015). *From project-based learning to artistic thinking: Lessons learned from creating an unhappy meal.* Lanham, MD: Rowman & Littlefield.

Wiggins, G., & McTighe, J. (2005). *Understanding by design* (2nd ed.). Alexandria, VA: ASCD.

Winebrenner, S., & Brulles, D. (2017). *Teaching gifted kids in today's classroom: Strategies and techniques every teacher can use* (3rd ed.). Minneapolis, MN: Free Spirit Publishing.

Wolpert-Gawron, H. (2014, June 19). How to design projects around common core standards [blog post]. Retrieved from *Edutopia* at www.edutopia.org/blog/how-to-design-projects-around-common-core-heather-wolpert-gawron

Wood, D., Bruner, J. S., & Ross, G. (1976). The role of tutoring in problem solving. *Journal of Psychology and Psychiatry, 17*, 89–100.

Zwiers, J., & Crawford, M. (2011). *Academic conversations: Classroom talk that fosters critical thinking and content understandings.* Portland, ME: Stenhouse.

Index

The letter *f* following a page number denotes a figure.

accountability
  encouraging, 89
  peer, reinforcing, 118–119
activities management. *See* Manage
  Activities
Align to Standards
  additional resources, 68, 79
  classroom example, 67–68
  determine which standards to focus
    on, 73–74
  for Gold Standard PBL, 6
  Gold Standard teaching practices,
    69
  instructional coaches, using, 76–78
  keeping the focus on learning
    goals, 74–75
  for meaningful learning, 70–73
  reasons for, 68–69
  rubric, continuum of criteria, 181
Align to Standards coaching methods
  driving questions gallery walk,
    76–77
  mind mapping, 76, 77*f*
  time line, 77–78
The Art of Coaching (Aguilar), 175
ask three before me routine, 95
Assess Student Learning
  additional resources, 106, 126
  clarifying assignments, 118
  classroom example, 104

Assess Student Learning—(*continued*)
  coaching activities, 124–125
  comprehensive approach, impor-
    tance of, 104–105
  for Gold Standard PBL, 7
  Gold Standard teaching practices,
    105
  grading strategies, 123–124
  milestone assignments, 114–115
  observe and question, 115
  peer accountability, reinforcing,
    118–119
  prior knowledge, 113–114
  reflection, encouraging, 119
  rubric, continuum of criteria,
    182–183
  rubrics, unpacking, 108–111
  striking a balance in, 106
  success skills, 21st century, 111–112
  without interrupting flow, 99
Assess Student Learning, formative
  assessment
  additional resources, 126
  defined, 106, 122
  mapping, 116, 117*f*
  timing, 106
Assess Student Learning, summative
  assessment
  defined, 106, 122
  forms, 122–123

Assess Student Learning, summative
  assessment—(continued)
    timing, 106
Assess Student Learning strategies
  balance individual and team
    assessment, 116–119
  feedback from multiple sources,
    encourage, 119–122
  formative assessment, emphasize,
    112–115
  success criteria, transparency
    about, 107–111, 110f
assignments, clarifying, 118
audiences
  feedback from, 120–121
  involving in projects, 60
authenticity
  Design and Plan, essential ele-
    ments, 47
  in Framework for High-Quality PBL,
    xv

balance in assessment, 106, 116–119
beliefs and values, sharing in culture
  building, 16–18, 36
bottlenecks, removing, 98–99
breaks, building in, 100
Buck Institute for Education (BIE), xvii,
  2, 39, 40
Build the Culture
  additional resources, 12, 37
  classroom example, 11–13
  for Gold Standard PBL, 6
  Gold Standard teaching practices,
    14
  importance for PBL, 13–14
  instructional coaches, using, 34–36
  rubric, continuum of criteria,
    180–181
  starting small, 31–34
  student's role in, 15
  teacher's role in, 15
  time and effort in, 15
Build the Culture coaching methods
  data collection, 35
  ghost walk, 35
  informal observations, 35–36
Build the Culture strategies
  beliefs and values, sharing core,
    16–18, 36

Build the Culture strategies—(continued)
  focus of, 15
  physical environment, 23–27, 25f,
    34
  protocols and routines, 27–31, 35
  shared norms, 18–23, 19f, 36
bulletin boards, digital, 97

calendars, flexibility in, 98
capacity building, xiv
Causes and Cures in the Classroom
  (Searle), 155–156
celebrations, 30, 173
check-ins, starting and stopping with,
  91
checklists, 93
choice
  Design and Plan, essential ele-
    ments, 48
  offering in coaching, 153
  student voice and, 48, 153
CISE, 45
Class Dojo, 97
classroom audit, 26–27
classroom culture. See Build the Culture
classrooms
  closing routines, 30
  digital, 97
  end-of-class routines, 30
  flexible, 23–24
  flipped model, 100
  morning meetings, 29–30
  physical environment, 23–27, 25f,
    34
  project walls, 24, 25f, 92–93, 169
  student-centered, habits for,
    27–31
clients, involving in projects, 60
closers, 30
cloud-based technology tools, 97
coaches
  capable, 161–162, 169
  teachers as, 161–163, 170–171
coaching methods. See also Engage
  and Coach
  Align to Standards, 76–78
  Assess Student Learning, 124–125
  Build the Culture, 34–36
  data collection, 35
  Design and Plan, 62–64

coaching methods—(continued)
  driving questions gallery walk,
    76–77
  ghost walk, 35
  informal observations, 35–36
  Manage Activities, 101–102
  mind mapping, 76, 77f
  time line, 77–78
collaboration
  in Framework for High-Quality PBL,
    xvi
  technology tools for, 96–97
collaboration, technology tools for,
  96–97
communication skills
  additional resources, 156
  scaffolding, 147
conferences, 163
continuous improvement, commitment
  to, xiv
contracts, teamwork, 89, 90f
cracking the case, 33
Creating Cultures of Thinking (Ritchhart), 35, 37
creativity
  additional resources, 92–93
  scaffolding, 147
Critical Exploration, 151
critique and revision in Design and
  Plan, 48
critique protocol, 28–29
Cultivating Curiosity in K-12 Classrooms
  (Ostroff), 175
Culturally Responsive Teaching and the
  Brain (Hammond), 37
culture, shaping schoolwide, 13. See
  also Build the Culture
curiosity, additional resources, 156, 175

data collection, 35
deadlines, 98
Design and Plan
  additional resources, 39, 66
  beginning, 39
  classroom example, 38, 48–50
  consult with experts, 50–51, 58, 59
  detail in, 51–53
  equity, designing for, 61–62
  flexibility in, 51–53
  for Gold Standard PBL, 6

Design and Plan—(continued)
  Gold Standard teaching practices,
    46
  impact, designing for, 61–62
  instructional coaches, using,
    62–64
  project calendars, 53, 54–57f
  refreshing projects, 64–65
  resources, 58–59
  reusing projects, 64–65
  rubric, continuum of criteria, 181
  technology tools, 58
Design and Plan, essential elements
  authenticity, 47
  challenging problem or question,
    47
  critique and revision, 48
  public product, 48–49
  reflection, 48
  student voice and choice, 48
  sustained inquiry, 47
Design and Plan, finding project ideas
  borrow, then adapt, 39–40
  build on your passions, 43
  codesign with students, 43–44
  connect to popular culture, 42
  listen to students, 41–42
  remodel old units, 40–41
  respond to requests, 42–43
  teach from the headlines, 42
Design and Plan, joining an existing
  project
  CISE, 45
  e-NABLE, 44
  iEARN, 44
  Out of Eden Walk, 45
Developing Natural Curiosity (Laur &
  Ackers), 156
differentiation
  additional resources, 156
  for inclusion, 139, 142
  as needed, 99
Differentiation in Middle School (Doubet
  & Hockett), 156
Differentiation in the Elementary Grades
  (Doubet & Hockett), 156
discussion protocols, 30
discussions
  need-to-know, 167–169
  structuring for inclusion, 142

Emodo, 97
employment
    contract, growth in, xi
    project-based, xi
    skills required, xi–xii
e-NABLE, 44
Engage and Coach
    additional resources, 158, 175
    celebrations, 173
    classroom example, 157–160
    for Gold Standard PBL, 7
    Gold Standard teaching practices,
        160–161
    the messy middle, 169–172
    at project launch, 163–167
    reflection, 173
    rubric, continuum of criteria, 184
English language learners, scaffolding
    for, 138–139, 140–141f, 143
entry events, 163–167
equity, designing for, 61–62
An Ethic of Excellence (Berger), 37
experts
    consulting with, 50–51, 58, 59
    feedback from, 121–122

feedback
    additional resources, 126
    expert, encouraging, 121–122
    from audiences, 120–121
    from multiple sources, 119–122
    gallery walks for, 28–29
    peer, soliciting, 119–120
fishbowl, 30
Fist to Five protocol, 146
formative assessment
    additional resources, 126
    defined, 106, 122
    emphasizing, 112–115
    mapping, 116, 117f
    timing, 106
The Formative Assessment Action Plan
    (Fisher & Frey), 126
From Project-Based Learning to Artistic
    Thinking (Werberger), 92–93

gallery walk, 28–29, 76–77
gestures to reinforce norms, 20
ghost walk, 35
Google Classroom, 97

Google Sites, 97
go with the flow, 99
grading, formative assessment vs.,
    112
grading strategies, 123–124
graphic organizers, 93, 143
Groups of Increasingly Larger Size
    (GOILS) protocol, 146
group work time, using strategically,
    99
G Suite for Education, 97

hand signals to reinforce norms, 20
homework, video lectures as, 100
How to Create and Use Rubrics for
    Formative Assessment (Brookhart),
    126
How to Differentiate Instruction in
    Academically Diverse Classrooms
    (Tomlinson), 156

Identity Safe Classrooms (Steele &
    Cohn-Vargas), 37
iEARN, 44
IEP goals, embedding into projects, 142
impact, designing for, 61–62
inclusion strategies
    combine wisdom, 139
    differentiate instruction, 139, 142
    discussions, structuring, 142
    IEP goals, embedding into projects,
        142
    learning strategies, modeling, 142
    offer workshops and mini-lessons,
        143
    prior knowledge, using, 142
    team up, 142
    technology, leveraging, 143
    visual aids, 143
    vocabulary, preteaching for inclu-
        sion, 143
Information Age companies, xi
innovation, culture of, xiii
inquiry
    Design and Plan, essential ele-
        ments, 47
    scaffolding, 151–152
Introduction to Student-Involved Assess-
    ment FOR Learning (Chappuis &
    Stiggins), 126

journals, 112
just-in-time scaffolding, 143–144, 170

Leaders of Their Own Learning (Berger, Rugan & Woodfin), 126
learning, personalized, 4–5
learning culture, xiii
Learning for Keeps (Koenig), 175
Learning Targets (Moss & Brookhart), 79
learning time, making the most of
    bottlenecks, removing, 98–99
    breaks, building in, 100
    deadlines, using, 98
    differentiate as needed, 99
    flip the classroom, 100
    go with the flow, 99
    group work time, use strategically, 99
    make calendars flexible, 98
    milestone assignments, 98
    reflection, find time for, 100
    workshop model, integrating the, 100–101
lectures, replacing with video, 100
lip dub music video, 33

Make Just One Change (Rothstein & Santana), 156
Manage Activities
    additional resources, 81, 103
    classroom example, 80–81
    coaching methods, 101–102
    in Framework for High-Quality PBL, xvi
    for Gold Standard PBL, 6–7
    Gold Standard teaching practices, 81–82
    instructional coaches, using, 101–102
    rubric, continuum of criteria, 182
    time management, 103
Manage Activities, making the most of learning time
    bottlenecks, removing, 98–99
    breaks, building in, 100
    deadlines, using, 98
    differentiate as needed, 99
    flip the classroom, 100

Manage Activities, making the most of learning time—(continued)
    go with the flow, 99
    group work time, use strategically, 99
    make calendars flexible, 98
    milestone assignments, 98
    reflection, find time for, 100
    workshop model, integrating the, 100–101
Manage Activities, teamwork
    accountability, encouraging, 89
    additional resources, 103
    check-ins, starting and stopping with, 91
    contracts, 89, 90f
    making the most of, 82–86, 85f
    mix up the dynamics, 91
    model desired behaviors, 89
    real-world examples, highlighting, 89–90
    reflection, encouraging, 91
    roles, assigning, 86–87, 88f
    for a strong start, 89
    takeaways, 102
Manage Activities, technology tools
    cloud-based, 97
    for collaboration, 96–97
    digital bulletin boards, 97
    digital classroom, 97
    project trackers, 97
    takeaways, 102
    wikis, 97
Manage Activities strategies
    checklists, 93
    digital project centers, 92
    graphic organizers, 93
    process wall, 101–102
    project folders, 92
    project walls, 92–93
    self-direction, encouraging, 95–96, 96f
    technology, integrating, 96–97
    time management, 98
    tools and routines, 91–95
mentors, involving in projects, 60
messy middle
    in Engage and Coach, 169–172
    evidence of the, 26
Microsoft 365, 97

milestone assignments, 98, 114–115
mind mapping, 76, 77*f*
mini-lessons for inclusion, 143
modeling
    desired behaviors, 89
    learning strategies for inclusion, 142
Monuments Project, 96–97, 150
morning meetings, 29–30

Never Work Harder Than Your Students and Other Principles of Great Teaching (Jackson), 103
Newsela, 133
norms, using shared in building culture, 18–23, 19*f*, 36
notebooks, interactive, 135

observations, informal, 35–36
Out of Eden Walk, 45

Padlet, 97
panel members, involving in projects, 60
PBL for 21st Century Success (BIE), 103
PBL in the Elementary Grades (BIE), 66
PBL Starter Kit (BIE), 66
PBworks, 97
peer accountability, reinforcing, 118–119
peer feedback
    additional resources, 126
    soliciting, 119–120
Peer Feedback in the Classroom (Sackstein), 126
physical environment in culture building, 23–27, 25*f*, 34
presentation skills, scaffolding, 147–150, 151*f*
Prioritizing the Common Core (Ainsworth), 79
prior knowledge, assessing, 113–114, 142
problems
    authentic, 59
    involving other adults, 59–60
problem-solving skills, scaffolding, 147
process wall, 101–102
product
    Design and Plan, essential elements, 48–49

product—(*continued*)
    in Framework for High-Quality PBL, xv–xvi
product users, involving in projects, 60
Project Assessment Maps, 116, 117*f*
Project Based Learning (PBL)
    additional resources, 2, 4, 66, 103
    benefits, 1
    Coaching Menu, 153, 154*f*, 155
    Framework for High-Quality, xiv–xvi
    Gold Standard, Essential Project Design Elements for, 3*f*, 49*f*
    reasons for, 1
    teacher's reflections on, 177–179
Project Based Learning (PBL) inclusion strategies
    combine wisdom, 139
    differentiate instruction, 139, 142
    imbed IEP goals into projects, 142
    introduce visual aids, 143
    leverage technology, 143
    model learning strategies, 142
    offer workshops and mini-lessons, 143
    preteach key vocabulary, 143
    structure discussions, 142
    tap prior knowledge, 142
    team up, 142
Project Based teaching
    conditions necessary for, xiii–xiv
    need for, xii–xiii
    personalized learning compatibility, 4–5
    practices for Gold Standard PBL, 5*f*, 6–7, 180–186
    shift to, 4
project calendars, 53, 54–57*f*
project centers, digital, 92
project design. *See* Design and Plan
project folders, 92, 110–111
project ideas, where to find good
    borrow, then adapt, 39–40
    build on your passions, 43
    codesign with students, 43–44
    connect to popular culture, 42
    listen to students, 41–42
    remodel old units, 40–41
    respond to requests, 42–43
    teach from the headlines, 42

project management. *See* Manage
    Activities
Project Management Toolkit for Teachers
    (Project Management Institute Educa-
    tional Foundation), 103
project trackers, 97
project walls, 24, 25*f*, 92–93, 169
protocols and routines
    ask three before me routine, 95
    Build the Culture strategies, 27–31,
        35
    celebrations, 30
    closing routines, 30
    critique protocol, 28–29
    discussion protocols, 30
    for effective meetings, 94–95
    employing, 91–95
    end-of-class, 30
    fishbowl, 30
    Fist to Five protocol, 146
    Groups of Increasingly Larger Size
        (GOILS) protocol, 146
    Manage Activities strategies, 91–95
    question protocols, 152
    reflections, 30
    Scaffold Student Learning, 145–146,
        151–152
    See/Think/Wonder, 92–93, 164
    thinking routines, 30

Question Formulation Technique (Right
    Question Institute), 151–152
question protocols, 152
questions
    additional resources, 151–152, 156
    coaching questions for teachers,
        173–174
    Design and Plan, essential ele-
        ments, 47
    driving, 166–167, 167*f*
    need-to-know, 148, 152, 166–167,
        167*f*

Real-World Projects (Boss), 66
reflection
    in Design and Plan, 48
    Design and Plan, essential ele-
        ments, 48
    encouraging, 91, 119
    find time for, 100

reflection—*(continued)*
    in Framework for High-Quality PBL,
        xvi
    post-project questions, 176–177
    at project end, 173
    protocols and routines, 30

    teacher's on PBL, 177–179
Reinventing Project Based Learning
    (Boss & Krauss), 103
Right Question Institute, 151–152
Rigorous PBL by Design (McDowell),
    126
roles, teamwork, 86–87, 88*f*
routines. *See* protocols and routines
rubrics
    additional resources, 126
    cocreating, 109
    as learning tools, 109–111
    unpacking in assessment, 108–109
rules vs. norms, 18

scaffolding teacher learning, 152–153,
    154*f*, 155
Scaffold Student Learning
    additional resources, 128, 155–156
    aligning to learning goals, 137–139
    disciplinary thinking, 150–153
    English language learners, 138–139,
        140–141*f*, 143
    for Gold Standard PBL, 7
    Gold Standard teaching practices,
        130
    The Great California Adventure
        classroom example, 127–128,
        130–132
    importance of, 128–130
    just-in-time, 143–144, 170
    protocols and routines, 145–146,
        151–152
    rubric, continuum of criteria,
        183–184
    student learning guides, using,
        132–133
    success skills, 145–149
Scaffold Student Learning,
    differentiating
    additional resources, 133
    content, 134–135
    process, 135

Scaffold Student Learning, differentiating—*(continued)*
  product, 136–137
Scaffold Student Learning, differentiation strategies
  interactive notebooks, 135
  learning stations, 134
  providing student options, 135, 136
School Climate Change (DeWitt & Slade), 37
school structures, redesigned/reimagined, xiii
See/Think/Wonder protocol, 92–93, 164
self-direction, encouraging, 95–96, 96*f*
self-management skills, 147–149, 170
sentence starters, 25
Setting the Standard for Project Based Learning (Larmer, Mergendoller, & Boss), 2
Slack, 97
So All Can Learn (McCarthy), 134–135, 156
standards. *See also* Align to Standards
  additional resources, 2
  power, 68
  priority, 68
starter projects, 31–34
Student Learning Guide (BIE), 132
student learning guides
  additional resources, 9, 132
  sample, 187–190
students
  in Framework for High-Quality PBL, xv
  help in project planning, 41–44
  self-assessment, 112
Students at the Center (Kallick & Zmuda), 66
Substitute, Combine, Adapt, Modify, Put to another use, Eliminate, Reverse (SCAMPER) scaffolds, 147
success criteria, transparency in, 107–111, 110*f*
success skills, scaffolding, 145–149
Success Starter, 11–12
summative assessment
  defined, 106, 122
  forms, 122–123
  timing, 106

Tasks Before Apps (Burns), 103
teachers
  as coaches, 161–163, 170–171
  coaching questions for, 173–174
  as warm demanders, 171–172, 172*f*
Teaching Gifted Kids in Today's Classroom (Winebrenner & Brulles), 156
Teaching in the Fast Lane (Rollins), 175
team planning guides, 147–148
team spirit, building, 34
teamwork
  activities for a strong start, 89
  assigning roles, 86–87, 88*f*
  check-ins, starting and stopping with, 91
  contracts, 89, 90*f*
  encourage accountability, 89
  highlight real-world examples, 89–90
  for inclusion, 142
  making the most of, 82–86, 85*f*
  mix up the dynamics, 91
  model desired behaviors, 89
  reflection, encouraging, 91
  routine for effective meetings, 94–95
technology
  for inclusion, 143
  integrating, 96–97
  tools for collaboration, 96–97
ThingLink, 49, 58
thinking routines, 30
time line, 77–78
time management, 98
transparency in success criteria, 107–111, 110*f*
Trello, 97
21st century skills, assessing, 111–112

Understanding by Design (2nd ed.) (Wiggins & McTighe), 79

video lectures as homework, 100
vision, xiii
visual aids, inclusion and, 143
vocabulary, preteaching for inclusion, 143

warm demanders, 171–172, 172*f*
Well Spoken (Palmer), 156
whiteboards, mini, 99
wikis, 97

wisdom, combining for inclusion, 139
workshop model, integrating the,
   100–101
workshops for inclusion, 143

About the Authors

Suzie Boss is a member of the Buck Institute for Education's National Faculty. She is a writer and educational consultant who focuses on the power of teaching and learning to improve lives and transform communities. She is the author or coauthor of several books on education and innovation, including *Setting the Standard for Project Based Learning, Real-World Projects, Bringing Innovation to School: Empowering Students to Thrive in a Changing World,* and *Reinventing Project Based Learning: Your Field Guide to Real-World Projects in the Digital Age.* She is a regular contributor to *Edutopia.* She collaborated with the award-winning Stephen Ritz to tell his inspiring story in *The Power of a Plant.* Her work has appeared in a wide range of publications, including *Educational Leadership, Principal Leadership,* the *New York Times, Education Week,* and *The Huffington Post.* She is a frequent conference presenter and consults internationally with schools interested in shifting from traditional instruction to technology-rich, Project Based Learning.

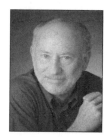

John Larmer is editor in chief at the Buck Institute for Education. He authored and/or edited BIE's project based curriculum units for high school government and economics and was a contributing author of the *Project Based Learning Handbook*. He is a coauthor of *Setting the Standard for Project Based Learning*, and he is a writer and editor of BIE's *PBL Toolkit Series*, including the *PBL Starter Kit for Middle and High School Teachers*, *PBL in the Elementary Grades*, and *PBL for 21st Century Success: Teaching Critical Thinking, Collaboration, Communication, and Creativity*. He codevelops professional development workshops and materials for teachers, including 21st century skills rubrics and project exemplars. John presents at conferences and has consulted on PBL curriculum development for the National Academy Foundation, the Oracle Education Foundation, and Pearson Education.

Prior to joining BIE, John was a senior program associate at WestEd in San Francisco. For 10 years John taught high school social studies and English. He was a founding teacher at a restructured small high school, a member of the National School Reform Faculty, and school coach for the Coalition of Essential Schools. John received MA degrees in educational technology and in educational administration from San Francisco State University, and a BA in political science from Stanford University.

BUCK INSTITUTE
FOR EDUCATION

The Buck Institute for Education (BIE) is a mission-driven, not-for-profit 501(c)3 organization based in Novato, California, and is beneficiary of the Leonard and Beryl Buck Trust. Since 1998, BIE has focused its work exclusively on Project Based Learning and is considered the world's leading provider of PBL resources and professional development. Its publications have been translated into nine languages. Across the United States and around the world, BIE provides PBL workshops and coaching to well over 10,000 K–12 teachers per year and provides systemic long-term support to partner schools and districts. BIE also hosts annual PBL World conferences and offers online resources at www.bie.org and online courses at PBLU.org.

Related ASCD Resources

At the time of publication, the following resources were available (ASCD stock numbers in parentheses).

Print Products

Creating a Culture of Reflective Practice: Capacity-Building for School-wide Success by Pete Hall and Alisa Simeral (#117006)

Everyday Problem-Based Learning: Quick Projects to Build Problem-Solving Fluency by Brian Pete and Robin Fogarty (#117057)

How to Create a Culture of Achievement in Your School and Classroom by Douglas Fisher, Nancy Frey, and Ian Pumpian (#111014)

Now That's a Good Question! How to Promote Cognitive Rigor Through Classroom Questioning by Erik M. Francis (#116004)

Reading, Writing, and Rigor: Helping Students Achieve Greater Depth of Knowledge in Literacy by Nancy Boyles (#118026)

Real-World Projects: How Do I Design Relevant and Engaging Learning Experiences? by Suzie Boss (#SF115043)

Setting the Standard for Project Based Learning: A Proven Approach to Rigorous Classroom Instruction by John Larmer, John Mergendoller, and Suzie Boss (#114017)

Transforming Schools: Creating a Culture of Continuous Improvement by Allison Zmuda, Robert Kuklis, and Everett Kline (#103112)

ASCD myTeachSource®

Download resources from a professional learning platform with hundreds of research-based best practices and tools for your classroom at http://myteachsource.ascd.org/

For more information, send an e-mail to member@ascd.org; call 1-800-933-2723 or 703-578-9600; send a fax to 703-575-5400; or write to Information Services, ASCD, 1703 N. Beauregard St., Alexandria, VA 22311-1714 USA.

WHOLE CHILD
TENETS

The ASCD Whole Child approach is an effort to transition from a focus on narrowly defined academic achievement to one that promotes the long-term development and success of all children. Through this approach, ASCD supports educators, families, community members, and policymakers as they move from a vision about educating the whole child to sustainable, collaborative actions.

Project Based Teaching relates to the **engaged** and **challenged** tenets. For more about the ASCD Whole Child approach, visit **www.ascd.org/wholechild.**

1 **HEALTHY**
Each student enters school healthy and learns about and practices a healthy lifestyle.

2 **SAFE**
Each student learns in an environment that is physically and emotionally **safe** for students and adults.

3 **ENGAGED**
Each student is actively engaged in learning and is connected to the school and broader community.

4 **SUPPORTED**
Each student has access to personalized learning and is supported by qualified, caring adults.

5 **CHALLENGED**
Each student is challenged academically and prepared for success in college or further study and for employment and participation in a global environment.